The
Hockey Goalie's Complete Guide

A FIREFLY BOOK

Published by Firefly Books Ltd. 2009

First printing

Publisher Cataloging-in-Publication Data (U.S.)

Allaire, François, 1955-
    The hockey goalie's complete guide / François Allaire.
[176] p. : col. ill., photos. (chiefly col.) ; cm.
Summary: Tips and techniques to improve a goalie's methods.
ISBN-13: 978-1-55407-476-1 (pbk.)
ISBN-10: 1-55407-476-2 (pbk.)
1. Hockey goalkeepers. I. Title.
796.96227 dc22   GV848.76.A453 2009

Library and Archives Canada Cataloguing in Publication

Allaire, François, 1955-
    The hockey goalie's complete guide / François Allaire.
Translation of: Devenir gardien de but au hockey.
Previously published in English under title: Hockey goaltending for young players.
ISBN-13: 978-1-55407-476-1
ISBN-10: 1-55407-476-2

    1. Hockey--Goalkeeping. 2. Hockey--Training. I.º Allaire, François, 1955- . Hockey goaltending for young players. II. Title.

GV848.76.A4413 2009   796.962'27   C2009-901246-4

Published in the United States by
Firefly Books (U.S.) Inc.
P.O. Box 1338, Ellicott Station
Buffalo, New York 14205

Published in Canada by
Firefly Books Ltd.
66 Leek Crescent
Richmond Hill, Ontario L4B 1H1

Printed in China

François Allaire

The Hockey Goalie's Complete Guide

○ ○ ○ An Essential
Development Plan

FIREFLY BOOKS

Acknowledgments

A very special thank-you to Yannick Garron of Boisbriand for allowing the use of the municipal arena to take the photos.

Additional thanks to Francis Desrosiers for his excellent demonstrations, his energy and his concentration while the photos were being taken.

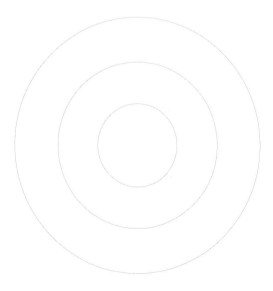

Table of Contents

Glossary

Symbols for Forwards

Offensive player	X
Defensive player	O
Forward motion	→
Backward motion	〜〜〜
Motion toward the puck	〜→
Pass	- - - →
Shot on goal	⇒

Symbols for Goalies

Goalie in the basic upright stance	
Goalie in the basic crouching stance	
Goalie in the basic butterfly stance	
Goalie in a blocking stance	
Kneeling to standing motion	
Motion to follow the rebound by rising up on the right leg	
Motion to follow the rebound by rising up on the left leg	
Motion to freeze the puck	
Motion with one pad on the ice, right post	
Motion with one pad on the ice, left post	

Stick motion on the ice, to the right	⊐⊏
Stick motion on the ice, to the left	⊐⊏
Forward motion while in the basic stance	♀
Backward motion while in the basic stance	⊿○
Forward motion while in the basic crouching stance	⊕
Backward motion while in the basic crouching stance	⊿⊖
T-motion to the right	○⌐
T-motion to the left	⌐○
Stopping	//
Watching the puck	○
Handling the puck	○〜»
Pass	○----»
Directing the puck to the right	○↗ ⇑
Directing the puck to the left	↖○ ⇑

Miscellaneous Symbols

Coach	*E*
Puck	●
Net	⌒⌒
Stick	╱

Introduction

Summary

1. Explain the stages of the development of a goaltender.

2. Explain the characteristics that differentiate the beginner goalie from a goalie who has completed the beginner level.

3. Explain and show in graphic form what a hockey season includes.

4. Explain and show in graphic form what a goalie development plan looks like.

	1	2	3	4
Period	Pre-season	Season	Post-season	Off-season
Month	J-A	S-O-N-D-J-F	M-A	M-J
A On-ice training		1. Skating techniques		
		2. Basic techniques		
		3. Three on-ice evaluations during this period		
B Off-ice training	I. Off-ice training sessions			II. Team sports
	II. Team sports	IV. Three off-ice evaluations during this period		III. Individual sports

ne of the greatest challenges facing a minor hockey coach is to train young goaltenders at the same pace as that of the other players on the team. The combined lack of experience on the part of the coach in this area, of time during training and of literature on this particular topic often means that the beginner goalie is an isolated member of the team. This book offers a development plan for beginner goalies.

But what exactly is a development plan? Simply put, it's a comprehensive plan that covers a period of four years. It contains information on skating techniques, basic moves, increasing physical fitness off the ice and evaluation methods, as well as several other topics that are essential to the development of a good beginner goalie.

The topics discussed in the final chapter represent, in general, the skills that a goalie coach needs to teach his goalies as they move up through the beginner's level (ages 9 to 12). However, deciding which coaching method to use (the number of practices, the learning rate, the order in which the various techniques are taught, the variety of exercises, etc.), is left up to the coach. All the coach needs to do is to ensure that as many of the items contained in this development plan as possible are taught before the age of 12. At this point, the goalie enters the intermediate phase. The coach, who is in constant contact with the team's goalies, remains the one individual best able to plan any specialized training for these goalies.

By offering a development plan (on the ice, off the ice, special exercises, etc.), this book is aimed not only at the people involved with novice, atom and peewee teams (coaches, parents, goalies), but also at the people involved with more advanced teams through the chapters dealing with observing, communicating, correcting, the roles of the goalie coach, and so on.

Many young goalies demonstrate remarkable talent. By using specific exercises to teach them what is important right from the start, they will get more enjoyment out of their favorite sport and achieve a greater level of skill.

There are three distinct phases in the career of a goalie who starts playing at the age of 9 and continues on into adulthood:

1st : the beginner goalie (ages 9 to 12)

2nd : the intermediate goalie (ages 13 to 16)

3rd : the advanced goalie (age 17 and up)

Each phase contains a certain number of skills that must be mastered in order to advance to the next phase. A goalie's development must be planned. The way to achieve this is to create a development plan that spans roughly four years, depending on the skill of the goalie. The purpose of this process is to reduce the element of luck as much as possible and to teach the beginner goalies the most important aspects of their role, namely:

1. Certain skating techniques (chapter 1)

2. Certain basic techniques (chapter 2)

3. Certain physical traits essential to the job of goalie (chapter 4)

Learning and applying these techniques and physical traits will help any young goalie just starting out in net to achieve the level of skill that is necessary to begin the intermediate step in the right direction.

Introduction

The following table lists the characteristics of a beginner goaltender and the characteristics of a goaltender who has completed the beginner phase.

Characteristics of a beginner goalie	Characteristics of a goaltender who has completed the beginner phase

— Has difficulty skating
  • lacks balance (falls frequently)
  • reacts slowly to the play
	— Can skate easily and quickly both inside and outside the crease

— Possesses few basic skills
  • awkward movements
  • difficulty performing different technical moves
  • makes the wrong choice regarding which basic technique to use
	— Possesses most of the basic skills necessary to be a goalie and uses them correctly

— Has difficulty stopping the puck
  • has difficulty judging shots made on net
  • allows several rebounds
  • often uses the wrong piece of equipment
	— Can easily stop most of the shots on goal

— Analyzes the game poorly • lacks playing experience	— Analyzes the play well and adapts accordingly

— Lacks confidence
  • deep in the net
  • often crouching on the ground
	— Gains confidence and now possesses a personal style

— Has difficulty with his equipment
  • too big or too heavy
  • provides inadequate protection
	— Can select equipment adapted to his needs and abilities

— Is in good physical condition generally	— Is sufficiently physically fit to begin more specialized training

1. Graphic representation of a hockey season

Table I shows a season as part of a development plan. The vertical columns divide the hockey season into periods and the corresponding months. The two types of training — on the ice and off — that are required as part of the development of a beginner goalie run in horizontal rows.

Table 1: The seasons

	1	2	3	4
Period	Pre-season	Season	Post-season	Off-season
Month	J-A	S-O-N-D-J-F	M-A	M-J
A **On-ice** **training**				
B **Off-ice** **training**				

Each season is divided into four distinct periods:

1. The pre-season (July and August), which focuses on the physical and psychological preparation of the beginner goalie for the coming season.

2. The season (September to mid-February), which focuses on the development of the beginner goalie's technical skill, while maintaining or improving the player's general physical fitness.

3. The post-season (mid-February to the end of April), which focuses on the specific preparation for the beginner goalie based on the opposing teams the goalie will face.

4. The off-season (May and June), which focuses on recovery (both physical and psychological), while maintaining the general physical fitness of the beginner goalie.

2. Completed graphic representation of a hockey season

For each of the four periods, there are things that the beginner goaltender must practice both on the ice and off. For example, skating techniques must be included in the on-ice training sessions from the start of September to the end of February. The Arabic numerals indicate the order of importance of each activity during on-ice training. The Roman numerals represent the same for off-ice training.

	1	2	3	4
Period	Pre-season	Season	Post-season	Off-season
Month	J-A	S-O-N-D-J-F	M-A	M-J
A On-ice training		1. Skating techniques		
		2. Basic techniques		
		3. Three on-ice evaluations during this period		
B Off-ice training	I. Off-ice training sessions			II. Team sports
	II. Team sports	IV. Three off-ice evaluations during this period		III. Individual Sports

The rest of this book will describe, one by one, the different activities included in each of the periods of the development plan for beginner goalies.

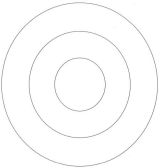

On-ice training

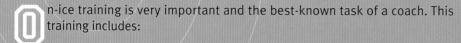

n-ice training is very important and the best-known task of a coach. This training includes:

• skating techniques
• basic techniques
• on-ice evaluation

To ensure the most complete training possible of young beginner goaltenders, some rules have to be set regarding the ideal frequency for on-ice training.

	1	2	3	4
Period	Pre-season	Season	Post-season	Off-season
Month	J-A	S-O-N-D-J-F	M-A	M-J
A On-ice training	F*: zero	F*: 4 times/week (90 minutes per training session) 1 or 2 games 1 or 2 training sessions (1 with the team; 1 with the city goalie school)	F*: 4 times/week (90 minutes per training session) 2 or 3 games (1 or 2 training sessions with the team)	F*: zero
B Off-ice training				

F*: The ideal training frequency that should be established for the on-ice training of the goalie during different periods of the hockey season.

1 Skating techniques

Summary

1. Emphasize the importance of skating for a beginner goaltender.

2. Describe what a goaltender gains from good skating ability.

3. Describe each of the skating techniques that a beginner goaltender needs to know.

	1	2	3	4
Period	Pre-season	Season	Post-season	Off-season
Month	J-A	S-O-N-D-J-F	M-A	M-J
A On-ice training		1. Skating techniques		
B Off-ice training				

Skating has long been recognized as the most important technical skill in hockey. As one of the players, the goaltender must also develop this skill and, more than any other player, develop it well, since this player is on the ice for the entire game.

The level of performance that a beginner goaltender can reach depends on the degree to which the goalie masters the skating techniques. In fact, a young goaltender who learns to skate well can achieve:

- good balance on skates;
- speed and agility on the ice, both of which are required to perform the moves with ease and accuracy.

These attributes will allow the goalie to:

- move faster;
- follow the puck better;
- move out of the goal;
- reduce fatigue during games and training;
- increase the player's ability to learn the basic techniques specific to the job of goalie;
- increase the player's confidence and motivation.

Through hard work and the proper teaching of skating techniques, any young goaltender will be able to achieve this level of performance. Therefore, it is important for the young goaltender to skate with the team during the training sessions, as well as on any other occasion that might arise, whether it is free skating, hockey school or skating on an outdoor rink.

Skating techniques

During practice, the coach should demand the best from the goaltender in terms of the technical moves in the same way that the coach does from the other players on the team. On the other hand, the goaltender's skating intensity and speed will be lower because of the weight of the equipment.

The following pages explain in detail each technical skating skill that a beginner goaltender needs to know. All the technical moves must be taught during the team's skating exercises. The goaltender must be included along with the other players. No special skating skills will be discussed in this chapter, since the goaltender must do the same skills training as the other players. Moreover, as far as skating is concerned, most coaches know enough to create exercises that encourage the goaltender to learn the skating techniques described in the following pages.

Forward start (Fig. 1 and 2)

- The goalie is standing. The skates are shoulder-width apart.

- The trunk and knees are slightly bent. The head is leaning forward.

- To start, the thrusting skate opens and the body leans forward, slightly unbalanced.

- The weight of the body is transferred over the thrusting skate and a vigorous push is produced at the hip and the knee of the thrusting leg.

- The initial three or four strides are short and quick.

Fig. 1

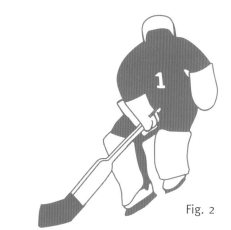

Fig. 2

Lateral start* (Fig. 3)

- The goalie is standing. To start, the head is turned in the desired direction and the body moves in the same direction, slightly unbalanced.

- The shoulders turn in the same direction and the outside leg crosses over the inside leg, thereby producing a push-off.

- The blade of the skate crossing over is placed perpendicular to the desired direction. The inside leg is brought forward to start the next push-off. At this point, this move resembles the forward start (see the first three points under "Forward start").

Fig. 3

Skating techniques

* This technical move must be performed on both the right and the left sides.

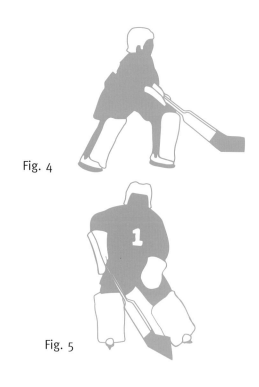

Fig. 4

Fig. 5

Forward skating (Fig. 4 and 5)

- After the start, skating forward means that the weight of the body is over the thrusting skate at the beginning of each push.

- The push-off is created by an energetic thrust at the hip and the knee is directed sideways and backward.

- The shoulders are perpendicular to the desired direction, the trunk is bent forward and the knee is beyond the end of the skate during the slide.

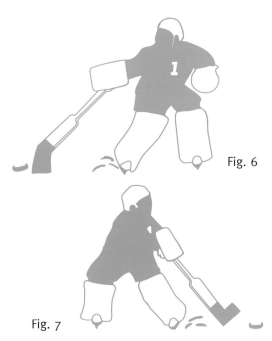

Fig. 6

Fig. 7

Outside skate stop* (Fig. 6 and 7)

- The goalie skating forward rotates the hips to place the outside skate blade perpendicular to the desired direction.

- The weight of the body rests on the forward section of the blade and the knee of this leg is bent to absorb part of the force.

- The inside leg stays back and does not participate in the stop. The trunk is bent forward and the stick is pointed in the same direction.

- Once the stop is completed, the goalie can easily initiate a backward start towards the net to return to the basic stance.

* This technical move must be performed on both the right and the left sides.

Forward skate crossover* (Fig. 8 and 9)

- The head and shoulders are turned to the middle of the circle. The trunk is bent forward.

- The weight of the body is over the inside skate that is pushing to the outside, while the outside skate is crossing over in front to become, in turn, the inside skate.

- The push-off is completed thanks to the front of the blades. The two legs alternate crossovers.

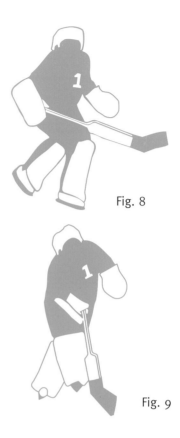

Fig. 8

Fig. 9

---

* This technical move must be performed on both the right and the left sides.

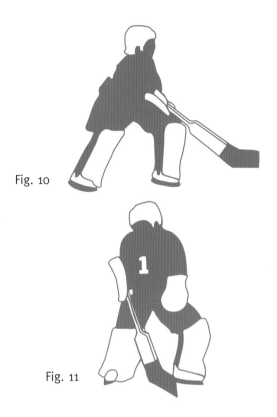

Fig. 10

Fig. 11

Pivot (forward skating to backward skating)* (Fig. 10 to 12)

- By slightly straightening the knees and the trunk, the two skates can be brought closer together. The weight of the body is placed over the skate opposite to the side to be pivoted.

- The head, shoulders and arms rotate on the side to be pivoted. The free leg is moved to the outside and the skate blade is placed at 180° to the other skate in the direction opposite to the skater and the other skate.

- The weight is then transferred to the leg that just pivoted. The other leg pivots and is placed parallel to the first leg. The skater can then skate backward.

Fig. 12

* This technical move must be performed on both the right and the left sides.

Backward start (Fig. 13 to 15)

- The goalie is standing. The weight of the body is transferred over the thrusting skate that is rotating to the inside in order to position the blade at 90° to the desired direction.

- There is an energetic thrust forward by the hip and the knee, then to the side, to make a curve on the ice surface.

- The weight of the body is then transferred to the other leg, creating another push-off.

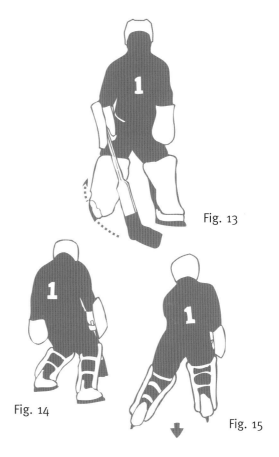

Fig. 13

Fig. 14

Fig. 15

Backward skating (Fig. 16)

- The goalie is crouching, the knees are bent and the trunk is leaning slightly forward.

- The body weight is transferred over the thrusting skate. An energetic thrust of the hip and the knee is made forward and to the side.

- During the push-off that creates a curve on the ice, the weight of the body is transferred over the other leg.

- The same move is alternately performed by each leg, creating two long "S"-shapes on the ice.

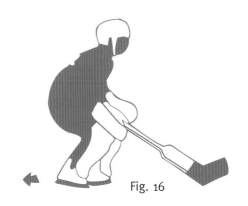

Fig. 16

Skating techniques

Fig. 17

Backward stop (one skate)* (Fig. 17)

- The body is leaning forward and the forward leg is completely bent.

- The rear skate is turned perpendicular to the direction of the player and the weight of the body is almost entirely on the rear leg.

- After having absorbed the force produced by the stop by bending the knee of the rear leg, the goalie can either return to the standing or basic stance or begin a forward or a backward start.

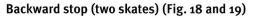

Fig. 18

Backward stop (two skates) (Fig. 18 and 19)

- The body is leaning quite far forward. The skates rotate to the outside and trace an arc that ends when the heels more or less touch each other.

- The weight of the body is over the end of the blades during the stop.

- Once the stop is completed, the blades are brought together, allowing the goalie to return to the standing or basic stance or to begin a forward or a backward start.

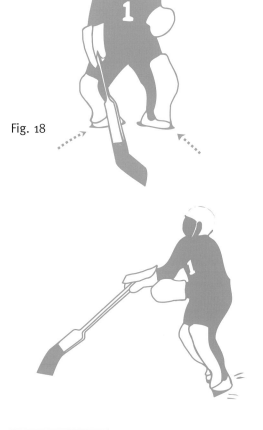

Fig. 19

The Hockey Goalie's Complete Guide

* This technical move must be performed on both the right and the left sides, and using each leg.

Backward skate crossover* (Fig. 20)

- The head, body and shoulders are turned to the inside of the circle, and the trunk is bent slightly forward.

- The outside skate pushes on the ice. At the same time, the weight of the body is transferred to the inside leg, which then pushes off.

- While the inside leg is pushing off, the outside leg is brought to the inside by placing it in front of the skate pushing off.

- At the end of the thrust, the inside skate is brought back to the middle of the circle by moving it behind the outside skate.

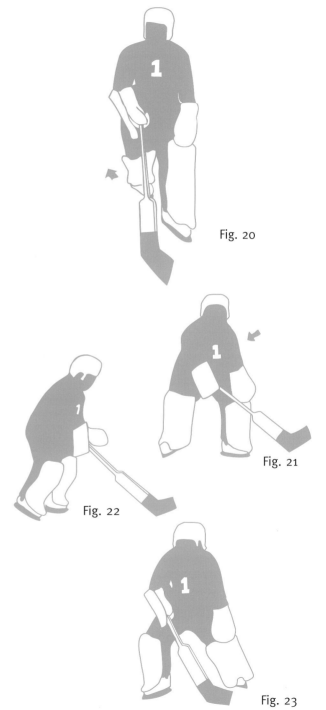

Fig. 20

Pivot (from backward skating to forward skating)* (Fig. 21 to 23)

- By slightly straightening the knees and bringing the skates closer together, the weight of the body is placed over the skate opposite to the side to be pivoted.

- The head, shoulders and arms rotate on the side to be pivoted. The free leg is lifted and moved to the outside in the desired direction.

- When the skate touches the ice, the other leg performs an energetic push-off. The skater can then skate forward.

Fig. 21

Fig. 22

Fig. 23

* This technical move must be performed using the right leg and the left leg.

2 Basic techniques

Summary

1. Explain the importance of learning the basic techniques during the beginner phase of goaltending.
2. Describe each of the basic techniques that a beginner goaltender needs to know.
3. Introduce specific exercises to develop each of the basic techniques described.
4. Briefly describe three concepts that the beginner goaltender must know.

	1	2	3	4
Period	Pre-season	Season	Post-season	Off-season
Month	J-A	S-O-N-D-J-F	M-A	M-J
A On-ice training		1. Basic techniques		
B Off-ice training				

Aside from the fact that a goaltender needs to learn the skating techniques, what most distinguishes the goalie from the other players on the team is the other basic techniques that this player has to master.

Unless a goaltender has freed the mind from all the technical considerations, the player cannot concentrate 100% on the game and on making quick decisions. It is appalling to see some goaltenders at the bantam (13–14 years old) or midget levels (15–16 years old) still having difficulty moving from the basic stance. At these levels where the game is played very quickly, the goaltender has to be able to master some of the basic techniques to be effective. Ideally, this type of learning should be encouraged in the initial phase of a goaltender's development (9 to 12 years old). At this stage, the game is not played very quickly. The young goaltender has an amazing ability to learn without having any automatic technical faults.

The following pages discuss the different basic techniques needed to allow the beginner goaltender to develop properly.

1

2

Basic stance

- The skates are spread more than shoulder-width apart. The opening between the pads is wider.
- The knees are bent and close to one another. This is practically a sitting position (photo 1).
- The trunk is bent far forward and the head is held high to observe the game (photo 2).
- The gloves are placed at knee level, but in front of the body so that they are within the goaltender's field of vision. Both elbows are bent and pointing forward.*
- The stick is placed between 12 and 16 inches (30 and 45 cm) away from the goalie.
- The weight of the body is firmly placed toward the front of the foot. The entire skate blade is in contact with the ice. However, the heel of the foot is slightly raised inside the boot.
- The stick should be gripped at the top of the paddle. The index finger is placed on the paddle, while the other fingers are placed around the shaft. This grip allows the goalie to better control the stick while making a save or while passing using only one hand (photo 3).

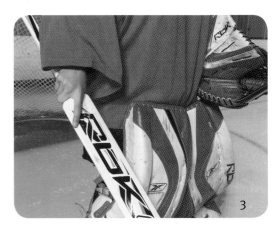

3

---

* The position of the gloves, which are placed within the field of vision of the beginner goaltender, appears to vastly improve coordination and the use of the catching glove.

Exercises to improve the basic stance

1. The goalie skates according to the coach's instructions, either in the basic stance or like a forward.

2. In the basic stance, the goalie places one knee on the ground, then reassumes the basic stance as quickly as possible. Alternate knees.

3. In the basic stance, the goalie goes around in a circle (360°), then reassumes the basic stance. Turn to the right and to the left.

360°

4. In the basic stance, the goalie crouches when the coach swings the stick near the head and jumps up when the stick swings under the skates. The goalie quickly reassumes the basic stance after every swing.

5. In the basic stance, the goalie lies on the stomach, then reassumes the basic stance as quickly as possible.

6. In the basic stance, the goalie moves to the right and to the left by crossing one leg over the other. The rest of the body maintains the basic stance.

7. In the basic stance, the goalie touches the ice behind him or her using one of the gloves, then reassumes the basic stance. Alternate gloves.

8. The goalie moves forward while maintaining the basic stance. Each time the player encounters a puck, the player jumps over it and reassumes the basic stance as quickly as possible.

9. The goalie maintains the basic stance while the coach or another goalie pushes him to try to make him lose his balance. After each push, the goalie must reassume the basic stance as quickly as possible.

1

2

Basic crouching stance*

- The skates are spread a little more than shoulder-width apart. The opening between the pads is a little wider (photo 1).
- The goalie's knees are quite bent. The position is almost a sitting position.
- The trunk is bent forward and is almost horizontal. The head is held high to observe the game properly.
- The player's gloves are placed at knee level but slightly in front of the knees. The player's elbows are completely flexed.
- The stick is placed 18 to 24 inches (45 to 60 cm) in front of the skates (photo 2).
- The weight of the body is almost over the toes.

---

* This technical move is used mostly during scrimmages in front of the net or during screened shots. Besides adopting this crouching position, the goalie must try to always follow the puck between the legs of the players during the game situations mentioned later.

- In the event of a screen, the goalie must maintain visual contact with the puck. To do this, the player must move the upper body to the right and to the left while keeping the legs and arms in the original basic stance as much as possible (photos 3 to 5).

3

4

5

Exercises to improve the basic crouching stance

1. The goalie skates according to the coach's instructions in the basic stance, crouching stance or like a forward.

2. In the basic crouching stance, the goalie watches the pucks by looking between the legs of the coach.

3. In the basic crouching stance, the goalie follows the movement of the puck.

4. Same exercise, but using a player or another goalie to screen the puck.

5. In the basic crouching stance, the goalie receives the shots coming from different directions and distances.

6. Same exercise, but using a player or another goalie to screen the puck.

7. Same exercise, but with two players to screen the puck.

Butterfly stance

- The entire length of each pad is touching the ice (photo 1).
- The trunk is upright and the buttocks are raised to cover as much of the area at the top of the net as possible. The head is held high to observe the play (photo 2).
- The gloves are placed at the side of the body.
- The stick is placed directly in front of the goalie.
- The weight of the body is placed over the knees.

Stopping pucks headed for the posts

- All the goalie needs to do is extend his pad on the side on which the puck is traveling (photos 3 and 4).
- The other pad remains back. When the puck is aimed at the center of the net, the goalie moves his equipment to the center (photo 5).

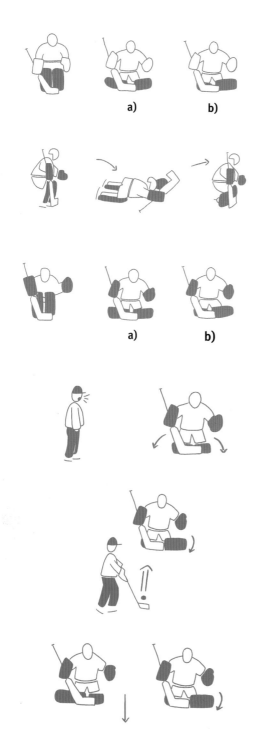

Exercises to improve the butterfly stance

1. Move from the basic stance to the basic butterfly stance:

a) Both pads are extended to the side.
b) One pad is extended to the side.

2. Move from the basic stance, then to flat on the stomach, then to the basic butterfly stance:

a) Both pads are extended to the side.
b) One pad is extended to the side.

3. Move from the basic crouching stance to the basic butterfly stance:

a) Both pads are extended to the side.
b) One pad is extended to the side.

4. The goalie is in the basic butterfly stance. The pads are extended back. According to the coach's instructions, the goalie:

a) extends the right pad to the side,
b) the left,
c) then both pads.

5. The goalie assumes the basic butterfly stance. Both pads are extended backward. Depending on the direction of the puck, the goalie moves the pad to the right or the left.

6. The goalie assumes the basic butterfly stance. The pads are extended backward. By alternately moving the pads to each side, the goalie is able to move forward.

7. Two goalies stand face to face. The goalie designated by the coach assumes the basic stance, the crouching stance or the butterfly stance with one or both pads extended to the side. The other goalie must react accordingly to copy the move.

Forward motion in the basic stance*

- The goalie assumes the basic stance.
- The goalie performs an outside rotation of the thrusting skate (approximately 90° to the desired direction).
- The weight is transferred over the thrusting skate and the thrusting leg is extended energetically backward from the hip and knee. The thrust produces a forward movement (photo 1).
- During the motion, only the thrusting leg should move. The rest of the body remains in the basic stance, which means the goalie is always ready to receive a shot.
- To stop, the goalie rotates the skate on the opposite leg to the inside to place the blade at 90° to the desired direction. The weight of the body is placed over the front of the blade.

    The goalie must be careful to keep his body facing the puck. Once the puck is stopped, the goalie must immediately reassume the basic stance (photo 2).

* This move is used to follow the puck during a pass from one player to another.

1

Backward motion in the basic stance

- The goalie is in the basic stance.
- The goalie performs an inside rotation of the thrusting skate (approximately 90° to the desired direction) (photo 1).
- The weight is transferred over the thrusting skate and the leg is extended vigorously from the hip and the knee as soon as the push-off is completed. The goalie reassumes the basic stance to start sliding backward.
- During the move, the upper body remains in the basic stance (photo 2).
- To make the save, the goalie rotates with only one skate to the outside at 90° to the direction in which the goalie is moving.
- As soon as the save is made, the goalie quickly reassumes the basic stance (photo 3).

2

3

Exercises to develop the forward and backward motions in the basic stance

1. Assume the basic stance. At the signal, the goalie quickly moves forward, then reassumes the initial position. Same thing backward.

2. Both goalies face each other at a distance of 6 feet (1.8 m). The goalie with the puck advances to pass it to the other goalie who, during this time, is retreating. The second goalie receives the pass, brakes, then begins advancing while the first goalie retreats.

3. In the basic stance, the goalie performs various moves in front of the goal.

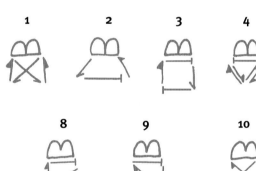

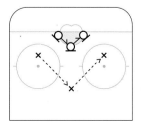
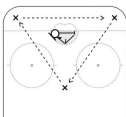
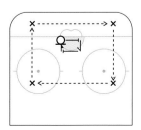
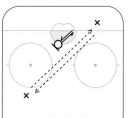

4. The goalie, in the basic stance, moves to follow the puck.

In the basic stance, the goalie moves to follow the puck in order to receive the shot.

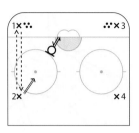

5. Player 2 passes to Player 1, who passes the puck back to Player 2, who then shoots. Next, Player 4 passes to Player 3, who then passes the puck back to Player 4, who shoots.

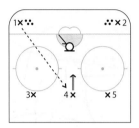

6. Player 1 passes to Player 3, 4 or 5, who then shoots at the goal. Next, Player 2 passes to Player 3, 4 or 5.

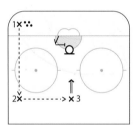

7. Player 1 passes to Player 2, who passes to Player 3, who shoots at the goal.

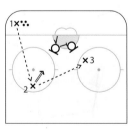

8. Player 1 passes to Player 2, who has the option to shoot at the goal or to pass to Player 3.

T-push and the basic stance while in motion*

- If the move is to the right, the goalie must first transfer the weight to the inside edge of the left skate (photo 1).
- Once the weight is transferred, a vigorous extension of the left leg allows the goalie to move to the right.
- The goalie opens the right skate to make it easier to move.
- The rest of the body remains in the basic stance during the entire move to always be ready to receive a shot.
- The identical but opposite move is used to travel from left to right (photos 2 and 3).

* This technical move is used to follow the puck.

Basic techniques

Exercises to improve the T-push and the basic stance while in motion

1. In the basic stance, the goalie follows the coach's instructions.

2. In the basic stance, the goalie arranges the four pucks to form a 6 foot (1.8 m) square.

3. In the basic stance, the goalie moves from one post to the other.

4. The two goalies face each other. The goalie designated by the coach moves either to the left or the right, in the basic stance. The other goalie must imitate these moves.

5. In the basic stance, the goalie follows the pass using a T-push.

6. In the basic stance, the goalie receives a shot from Player 1. Player 1 passes to Player 2, who then shoots.

7. The goalie, in the basic stance, receives a shot from Player 1 as the player approaches. Right after this, Player 2, who remains stationary, fires a shot.

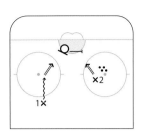

8. In the basic stance, the goalie receives the shots from the players organized in a particular order.

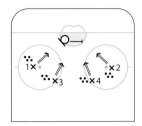

9. In the basic stance, the goalie receives the shots from the players organized in a particular order.

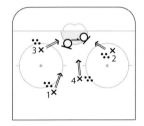

Freezing the puck

- The goalie is standing in the basic stance.
- When the puck is near the goalie, or when the goalie has just allowed a rebound, the goalie can kneel on both knees.
- The goalie places the catching glove on the puck, as well as the stick or the blocker to avoid having an opposing player take the puck away (photo 1).
- When the goalie is in the basic butterfly stance, the move is the same.
- If the goalie has to dive on to the stomach to freeze the puck, the goalie must try the same move again, while being careful not to push the puck forward or to have it slide underneath the body (photo 2).
- Whatever the situation, the goalie must keep the head up high and eyes open to watch the opposing players, the gloves and, of course, the puck.

1

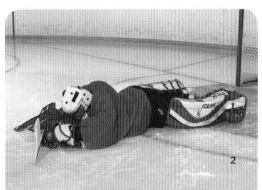

2

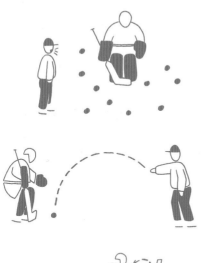

Exercises to develop the puck covering technique

1. The goalie is in the basic stance. Several pucks are spread out around the goalie. According to the coach's instructions, the goalie must cover one of the pucks.

2. The coach tosses a puck near the goalie. Once a puck touches the ice, the goalie must cover it.

3. In the basic stance, the goalie juggles the puck. Once the puck falls to the ice, the goalie must cover it.

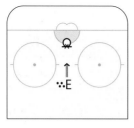

4. The coach moves the puck close to the goalie. When the goalie thinks there is a chance, the player tries to cover the puck.

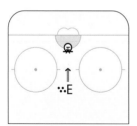

5. In the basic stance, the goalie blocks, then covers the pucks being shot.

6. In the basic butterfly stance, the goalie blocks, then covers the pucks being shot. For each of these exercises, the goalie can cover the puck:

— while down on both knees,
— flat on the stomach on the ice.

Kneeling to standing motion

- The goalie is in the basic butterfly stance (photo 1).
- The goalie lifts one leg and places the skate blade on the ice (photos 2 and 3).
- The goalie immediately returns to the basic stance (photo 4). During this move, the gloves, stick and head must remain stationary; only the legs move.
- The goalie must practice this move using the right leg and the left leg equally (photos 2 and 3).

1

2

3

4

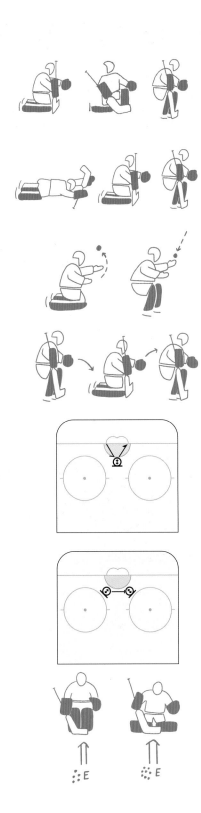

Exercises to develop the use of the knees to stand up

1. In the basic butterfly stance, the goalie lifts the left leg and returns to the basic stance. The goalie performs the same move on the right side.

2. The goalie lies on his or her stomach. The goalie rises up on one knee, then reassumes the basic stance.

3. In the basic butterfly stance, the goalie throws a ball into the air. The goalie reassumes the basic stance to catch the ball.

4. In the basic stance, the goalie crouches to assume the basic butterfly stance, then stands up again to reassume the initial position.

5. In the basic stance, the goalie moves forward, stops, assumes the basic butterfly stance, stands up, then moves backward.

6. In the basic stance, the goalie moves to the right, assumes the basic butterfly stance, stands up and moves to the left.

7. In the basic stance, the goalie receives a high shot followed by a low shot that has to be blocked with the pads, and so on.

Motion to follow the rebound using the correct leg

- When the rebound is far away to the right of the goalie, the goalie stands up using the left leg and pushes off in the direction of the puck (photo 1).
- The right skate is pointed in this direction and, as soon as the goalie is at the top of the crease he reassumes the basic stance.
- The goalie has now assumed the basic stance and is ready for a shot or a new pass (photo 2).
- The identical but opposite move is used to follow the rebound on the left side (photos 3 and 4).

1

2

3

4

5

- If the rebound is far away, yet near an opposing player who could immediately shoot at the goal, the goalie performs the same move, but remains on the ice (photos 5 to 8).
- The goalie is now in the basic butterfly stance, ready to receive a new shot.

6

7

8

Exercise to develop the motion to follow the rebound using the correct leg

1. In the basic butterfly stance, the goalie stands the right leg up and pushes to the left to the top of the crease to reassume the basic stance. The goalie performs the same move on the other side.

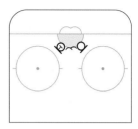

2. In the basic butterfly stance, the goalie pushes off the right leg and moves to the top of the crease on the left side to reassume the basic blocking position (see page 76). The goalie performs the same move on the other side.

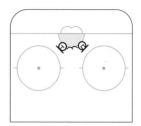

3. In the basic stance at the post, the goalie pushes off toward the top of the crease and assumes the butterfly stance. The goalie stands the right leg up and pushes off to the top of the crease on the left side to reassume the basic stance. The goalie performs the same move on the other side.

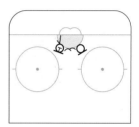

4. In the basic stance at the post, the goalie pushes off toward the slot, assumes the basic butterfly stance, stands the right leg up and pushes off to the top of the crease on the left side to reassume the basic stance. The goalie then receives a shot from Player 1. The goalie performs the same move on the other side.

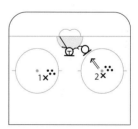

5. In the basic stance at the post, the goalie pushes off toward the slot, assumes the basic butterfly stance and pushes off the right leg toward the left post to reassume the basic blocking stance (see page 76). The goalie receives a shot from Player 1 and performs the same move on the other side.

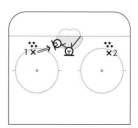

Intercepting the puck coming from a corner of the rink

- The goalie is positioned beside the goal post. The skate and the pad are pressed against the post (photo 1).
- The goalie's body is facing forward, away from the net, while only the head is looking back. The knees are bent and the skates are parallel in order to quickly move forward or to the opposite post.
- The stick is placed beside the net as close as possible to the goal line.
- The goalie must be ready to deflect the puck or to stop it by bending or by extending the arm holding the stick.
- The catching glove is held open outside the net to catch any high passes (photo 2).
- If the puck is directed at the other side of the net, the goalie quickly moves to the other post to assume the same position.

1

2

Exercises to develop the ability to intercept the puck coming from a corner

1. Positioned near the post, the goalie blocks the pucks shot in that direction by the players. The goalie can:
— block and return the puck behind the net,
— block and cover the puck.

2. Positioned near the post, the goalie blocks the pucks shot in that direction by the moving players. The goalie can:
— block and return the puck behind the net,
— block and cover the puck.

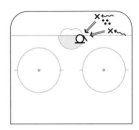

3. Positioned near the post, the goalie blocks the pucks shot in that direction. If the block fails, a player positioned in front of the net can take a shot on goal.

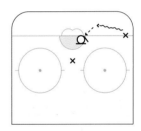

4. The goalie, positioned near the post, monitors the movement of Player 1, who tries to pass the puck to Player 2 in front of the goal.

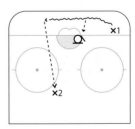

Observing the puck behind the net

- The goalie is in the basic stance, very close to the goal line.
- The goalie is bending a little more than normal to move quickly depending on the direction taken by the opposing player (photo 1).
- Only the head is turned in the direction of the puck. If the puck is to the right of the central post of the net, the goalie turns the head to the right and moves in that direction. If the puck is to the left of the central post, the goalie turns the head to the left and moves in that direction (photos 2 and 3).
- When the player tries to pass the puck or materializes in front of the net, the goalie assumes the same position as if trying to block the puck coming from a corner of the rink (see the previous technique) (photo 4).

1

2

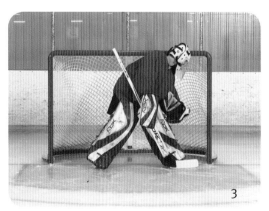
3

4

Two mistakes are frequently made when watching the puck behind the net.

5

6

The goalie turns to the back of the goal.

The goalie spreads the legs too far apart and is unable to push off during a pass.

Exercises to develop the ability to monitor the puck behind the net

1. The goalie must observe and move in relation to the player who is skating with the puck behind the net.

2. The goalie must observe and move in relation to the movement of the puck.

3. The goalie must observe and move in relation to the movement of the puck.

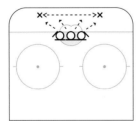

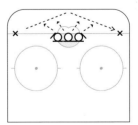

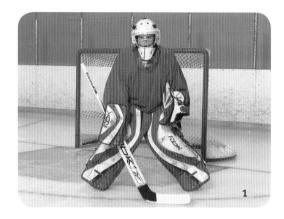

Motion behind the net (catching glove side)

- The goalie is in the basic stance and is watching the player located in the neutral zone (photo 1).
- When the puck is shot in along the boards, the goalie moves to face the play, opens the skate nearest the boards and pushes off with the opposite leg (photo 2).
- Now close to the boards, the goalie reassumes the basic stance and places the stick at an angle along the boards to stop the puck (photo 3).
- When the puck is stopped, the goalie returns to the net as quickly as possible by opening the skate nearest the net and by pushing off on the opposite leg (photo 4).
- Once he has returned to the same side of the net, the goalie assumes the same position used to block the puck coming from the corner (photo 5).

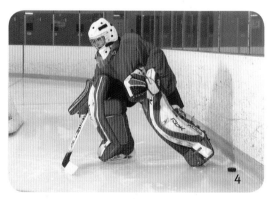

Motion behind the net (blocker side)

- The procedure is the same except that when the player is close to the boards, the goalie can either place the stick along the boards (photo 3) or stop the puck with a skate (photo 4).

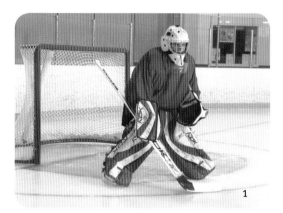

1

2

3

4

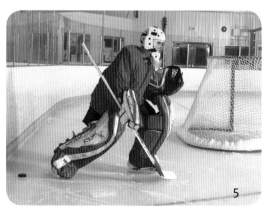

5

6

Basic techniques

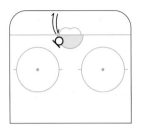

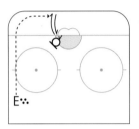

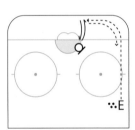

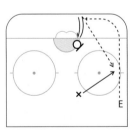

Exercises to develop the technique of playing the puck behind the net

1. The goalie is in the basic stance at the top of the crease. The goalie heads toward the boards to touch them with the stick and retreats immediately to the net.

2. The goalie is in the basic stance at the top of the crease. When the coach shoots the puck along the boards, the goalie leaves the net to stop it. If the goalie anticipates the play, the coach can shoot the puck toward the net.

3. The goalie is in the basic stance at the top of the crease. When the coach shoots a puck along the boards, the goalie leaves the net to stop it and returns the puck in the same direction.

4. When the player shoots a puck along the boards, the goalie leaves the net to stop it and passes it along the boards to one of the players.

Two-handed puck handling

- The goalie skates in the basic stance.
- The goalie places the blocker at the top of the shaft and the catching glove at the top of the paddle (photo 1).
- The shoulders and arms must be relaxed and the elbows held away from the body (photo 2).
- The goalie pushes the puck to one side. Next, the blade of the stick is quickly placed on top of the puck to stop it. The puck is then pushed in the opposite direction and the preceding steps are repeated.
- The side dribble (the goalie dribbles the puck at his or her side) offers the greatest advantage to the goalie, for it is fairly easy to learn and to fire off a pass.
- The stick can also be gripped by reversing the grip of the catching glove (photos 3 and 4).

1

2

3

4

Exercises to develop two-handed puck handling*

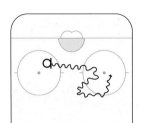

1. The goalie stickhandles the puck using both hands when skating forward or backward.

2. In the basic stance, the stationary goalie stickhandles a medicine ball using two hands.

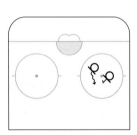

3. A goalie stickhandles the puck inside a face-off circle. A partner follows the goalie to try to take away the puck.

4. The goalie stickhandles the puck through a course marked by pylons. The goalie can stickhandle the puck while skating forward or backward.

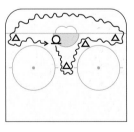 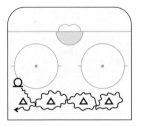 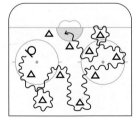

The Hockey Goalie's Complete Guide

* Each exercise can be performed using the conventional grip or the reversed grip.

One-handed backhand pass

- The goalie is in the same position as for playing the puck behind the net. The puck is then brought around on the right side (for a goalie wearing the blocker on the right hand), at roughly skate level (photo 1).
- The stick shaft is pressed against the goalie's back and the puck is touching the stick blade.
- The weight of the body is over the skate nearest to the puck.
- The blade of the stick must be at 90° to the desired direction. The goalie sweeps the puck, shifting all of the weight onto the stick.
- Once the puck leaves the blade of the stick, the stick follows through in the direction of the puck towards the desired target.

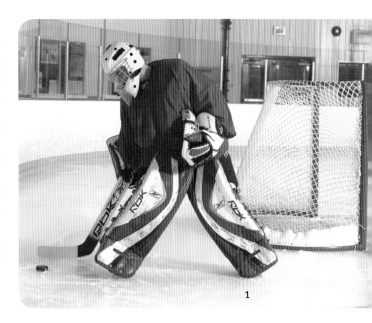

1

Two-handed pass from the right*

- The goalie is in the same position used for two-handed stickhandling. The puck is brought to the side while remaining in contact with the stick blade, which is slightly angled (photo 1).
- The weight of the goalie's body is over the skate on the same side as the puck. The goalie sweeps the puck toward the target, shifting the weight onto the stick.
- The blade of the stick must be at 90° to the desired direction. Once the puck leaves the blade of the stick, the stick follows through the direction of the puck toward the target. The goalie must keep the elbows pointed away from the body (photo 2).

1

2

---

* The shots are not discussed for beginner goaltenders, since most of them do not have the muscle strength necessary to carry out this technical move. Therefore, they have to be content with stickhandling and passing the puck, as described earlier.

Basic techniques

3 4

- The stick can be gripped with one hand reversed. For many goalies, passes are more accurate using this position (photos 3 and 4).

Exercises to develop a one-handed or a two-handed pass*

1. The goalie must pass the puck between the pylons placed at different locations on the ice.

2. The two goalies face each other. When the goalie with the puck advances with it, the partner retreats. Once the pass is made, the goalie who now has the puck advances and the partner retreats.

3. In the basic stance, the goalie receives the shot. Once the goalie has stopped the puck, the goalie executes a pass to the coach.

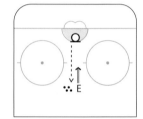

4. One goalie skates while stickhandling the puck, which the goalie then passes to the partner.

5. The goalie moves forward, grabs a puck and executes a pass to the coach, who can move around the ice. Once the pass is made, the goalie returns to the goal.

6. In the basic stance, the goalie receives a shot. Once the goalie has stopped it, the goalie executes a pass to a player who is moving around the ice.

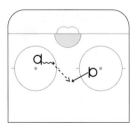

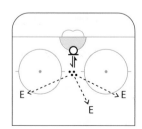

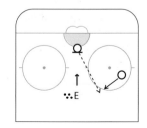

* For each of these exercises, the goalie can pass the puck with one hand or two, using the conventional or the reversed grip.

Techniques for stopping the puck*

The goalie, regardless of age and ability, must face the following types of shots:
– low shots,
– mid-height shots,
– high shots.

Moreover, these shots can be fired:
– to the right side of the net,
– to the center of the net,
– to the left side of the net.

As a result, the task of the goalie is to:
– control (e.g., using the catching glove);
– redirect (e.g., using the stick);
– or absorb the puck (e.g., using the trunk).

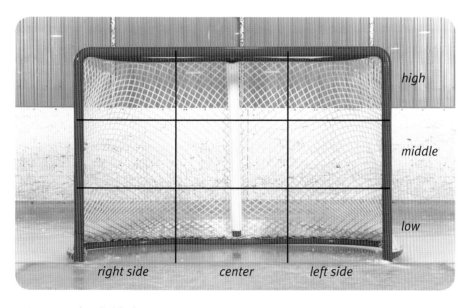

A net can be divided into nine specific zones.

The order (right side, left side) corresponds to the position of the goalie standing in front of the net.

Various save techniques using the following equipment apply to each of these zones.

---

* For all save techniques, the angle from which the shot is coming, the type of shot and the strength of the shot should often vary during the shooting exercises.

1. Save techniques for low shots

A. *Save using pads*
   Height: low shot
   Direction: to the right side or left side of the net
   Task: direct or absorb

- The goalie is in the basic butterfly stance (photo 1).
- The goalie can direct the puck into the corner by sliding the pad in the desired direction or absorb the puck by placing the pad perpendicular to the direction of the puck. The goalie must immediately freeze the puck using the catching glove.
- The goalie keeps the eyes on the puck until the puck comes in contact with the pad (photo 2).
- The goalie can use the basic butterfly stance with both legs extended or only one leg extended to the side to which the puck is heading (photo 3).

Exercises to develop the save technique using pads (low shots)

1. In the basic butterfly stance, the goalie directs the puck to the corner of the rink using the pads.

2. The goalie can also assume the basic stance, execute the save using the basic butterfly stance and reassume the initial position between each shot.

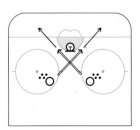

B. *Save using knee pads*
  Height: low shot
  Direction: to the center of the net
  Task: absorb or guide the puck in front.

- The goalie is in the basic butterfly stance (photo 1).
- The goalie brings the knees as close together as possible toward the center. The goalie can do this by bringing the skates closer together, which helps the knees close up (photos 2 and 3).
- Following the save, the goalie tries to take possession of the rebound using the stick and to hold the puck using the gloves.
- The goalie keeps the eyes on the puck until it comes in contact with the knee pads or the pants (photo 4).*

Exercises to develop the save technique using knee pads (low shots)

1. In the basic butterfly stance, the goalie tries to absorb the puck or to guide it in front.

2. The goalie can also be in the basic stance, execute the save in the basic butterfly stance and reassume the initial position between each shot.

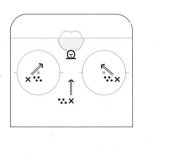

---

* Top-quality knee pads are mandatory to properly execute this move.

2. Save techniques for mid-level shots*

A. *Save using the catching glove*
   Height: mid-level shot
   Direction: to the right side or the left side, depending on the hand using the catching glove
   Task: control the puck

- The goalie is in the basic stance (photo 1).
- When the shot is fired, the goalie assumes the basic butterfly stance and moves the catching glove toward the puck to catch it in front of the body (photo 2).
- The goalie must hold the puck until it is firmly inside the catching glove (photo 3).

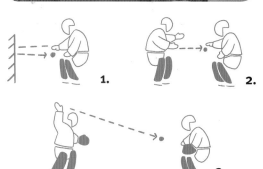

Exercises to develop the save technique using the catching glove (mid-level shots)

1. In the basic stance or butterfly stance, the goalie throws a ball against the boards and catches it using bare hands.

2. Facing each other while in the basic or butterfly stance, the two goalies throw a ball to each other.

3. Facing each other while in the basic or butterfly stance, the two goalies throw a puck to each other, using their catching glove to catch it.

4. In the basic stance, the goalie switches to the basic butterfly stance when the shot is fired and catches the puck using the catching glove.

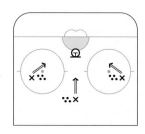

---

* Beginner goalies who are not tall enough to cover the entire area of the net should remain standing to catch high shots to the corners of the net.

B. *Save using the blocker*
  Height: mid-level shot
  Direction: to the right side or the left side, depending on the hand using the catching glove
  Task: guide the puck

- The goalie is in the basic stance (photo 1).
- During the shot, the goalie goes into the basic butterfly stance and moves the blocker toward the puck to make contact in front of the body (photo 2).
- The goalie must watch the puck until it touches the blocker.
- By flexing the wrist toward a corner of the rink, the goalie can aim the puck in that direction, if time and the strength of the shot allow (photo 3).

Exercises to develop the save technique using the blocker (mid-level shots)

1. In the basic stance, the goalie juggles the puck that rebounds off his blocker.

2. Facing each other, the two goalies shoot the puck back and forth to each other, taking turns using their blocker in the basic stance or in the basic butterfly stance.

3. In the basic stance, the goalie assumes the basic butterfly stance when the shot is fired and directs the puck to a corner of the rink.

1.

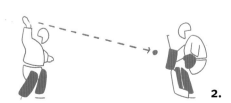

2.

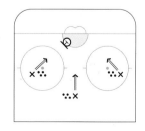

3.

1

2

3

C. *Save using the upper body*
   Height: mid-level shot
   Direction: to the center of the net
   Task: absorb

- The goalie is in the basic butterfly stance. The goalie should not be sitting on the skates because the goalie must cover as much area as possible at the top of the net (photo 1).
- The goalie must absorb, not hit, the puck with the body. Once the goalie has made contact with the puck, the goalie can try to hold it using one or both arms (photo 2).
- Or, the goalie can let the puck fall on the ice and hold it using his gloves.
- The goalie must watch the puck until it is completely immobilized in the arms or gloves (photo 3).

Exercises to develop the save technique using the upper body (mid-level shots)

1. In the basic butterfly stance, the goalie receives the pucks being shot by the coach.

2. In the basic butterfly stance, the goalie receives the tennis balls being shot by a player.

3. In the basic stance, the goalie faces Player 1. Player 1 passes to Player 2, who shoots at the center of the net at about mid-height. The goalie moves and, during the shot, assumes the basic butterfly stance to execute the save.

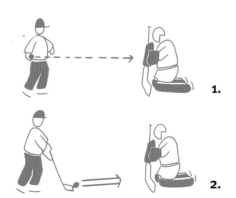

1.

2.

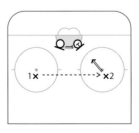

3.

3. Save techniques for high shots

A. *Stop using the catching glove*
Height: high shot
Direction: to the right side or the left side, depending on the hand using the catching glove
Task: control the puck

- Same move as the save using the catching glove at mid-height, except that it is higher (photo 1).
- Everything depends on the height of the goalie and the strength of the shot; the goalie can remain in the basic stance or make the save in the basic butterfly stance (photos 1 and 2).

Exercises to develop the save technique using the catching glove (high shots)*

1. The proposed exercises to develop the save technique using the catching glove against mid-level shots can also be used for high shots.

* Beginner goalies who are not tall enough to cover the entire net may prefer to remain standing to catch the high shots to the corners of the net.

B. *With the blocker*
Height: high shot
Direction: to the right side or the left side of the net, depending on the hand using the catching glove
Task: direct or control the puck

- Everything depends on the height of the goalie and on the strength of the shot; the goalie can remain in the basic stance or make the save in the basic butterfly stance (photos 1 and 2).
- Same move as the save using the blocker at mid-height, except the blocker is higher (photo 2).

Exercises to develop the save technique using the blocker (high shots)*

1. The exercises proposed to develop the save technique using the blocker against mid-level shots can also be used for high shots.

---

* Beginner goalies who are not tall enough to cover the entire net may prefer to remain standing to catch the high shots to the corners of the net.

C. *Save using the upper body*
   Height: high shot
   Direction: center of the net
   Task: absorb and control the puck

- Same move as the save using the upper body for mid-level shots.
- The goalie must keep the arms tight to the body to prevent any opening between the trunk and the arms (photo 1).
- For this kind of save, it may be better for the goalie to hold the puck against the stomach using one or both arms and to assume the basic butterfly stance to avoid having the puck fall on the ice (photo 2).

Exercises to develop the save technique using the upper body

1. The exercises proposed to develop the save technique using the upper body against mid-level shots can also be used against high shots.

SPECIAL SITUATIONS

Over the years, new moves have appeared to help goalies in special situations.

1. Save technique with one knee on the ice

- The goalie is in the basic stance at the post (photo 1).
- During a shot coming from a very tight angle, the goalie can use the forward motion with one knee on the ice (photo 2).

3

- The goalie turns the skate nearest the post in the direction of the corner of the rink (photo 3).
- The goalie places one pad on the ice as closely as possible to the skate nearest the post (photo 4).
- The goalie uses the post as a support by pressing the elbow and glove against it (photo 5).
- The move is the same on the other side (photos 6 to 9).

4

5

6

7

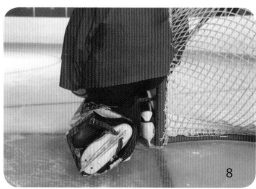

8

9

Exercises to develop the save technique with one knee on the ice

1. The goalie starts in the basic stance at the post. The goalie turns the skate nearest the post toward the corner of the rink and uses his hand and the elbow for support.

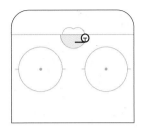

2. The goalie starts in the basic stance at the top of the crease. The goalie pushes off toward the post and uses the save technique with one knee on the ice.

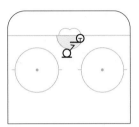

3. The goalie is in the basic stance at the post. The coach shoots between the legs and the goalie uses the save technique with one knee on the ice. The goalie must wait for the shot before making a move.

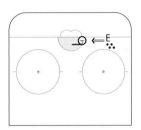

4. The goalie is in the basic stance at the top of the crease. The goalie pushes off toward the post. Once the goalie reaches the post, the coach shoots between the goalie's legs. The goalie uses the save technique with one knee on the ice.

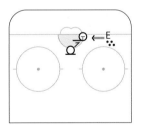

5. The goalie is in the basic stance at the post. The goalie moves from one post to the other. Once the goalie is at the other post, the coach shoots the puck between the goalie's legs. The goalie uses the save technique with one knee on the ice.

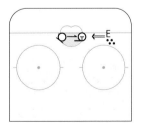

2. Save technique with the stick on the ice

- The goalie is in the basic stance at the post (photo 1).
- When the player goes around the net and tries to score near the post, the goalie crouches and places a pad just inside the post (photo 2).
- The goalie lays the stick flat on the ice, perpendicular to the pad. The free hand helps freeze the puck after the save (photo 3).
- The goalie makes the same move with the stick on the other side, while keeping his free hand ready to freeze the puck (photo 4).

Exercises to develop the save technique with the stick on the ice

1. The goalie starts in the basic stance and makes the move on one side. The goalie stands up, moves to the other post and makes the same move on the other side.

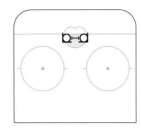

2. In the basic stance, the goalie stops the puck with the stick on the ice as the coach tries to score from behind the net. The goalie practices this move on both sides.

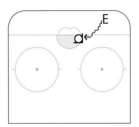

3. In the basic stance in the center of the net, the goalie moves to the post and stops the puck with the stick on the ice when the player tries to score near the post. The goalie practices this move on both sides.

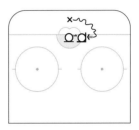

4. In the basic stance, the goalie moves from one post to the other and stops the puck with the stick on the ice when the player tries to score by going around the net. The goalie practices this move on both sides.

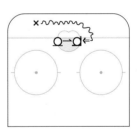

3. Block save technique

- When the play takes place close to the goal, the goalie uses this move (faking an opponent out of position) to do a block save (photo 1).
- During this play, the goalie pushes off and goes to the ice by bringing the arms to the sides and his knees as close together as possible (photo 2).
- Note that in order to make this motion, the goalie must keep the stick away from the body, otherwise an opening will be created between the body and the arm (photo 3).
- The goalie can move the feet closer together to help close the knees (photo 4).
- To perform this technique successfully, the goalie has to be able to perform the block save as close to the player's stick as possible and allow him or herself to be hit by the puck.

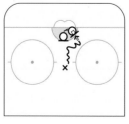

Faking

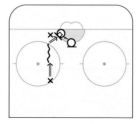

Deflection

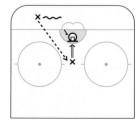

Pass in the goal

Exercises to develop the block save technique

1. In the basic stance at the top of the crease, the goalie blocks in the direction of the post.

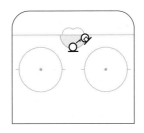

2. In the basic stance at the top of the crease, the goalie moves to make the block at the post when the coach does a deke on the catching glove side. The goalie practices this move on both sides.

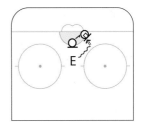

3. In the basic stance at the top of the crease, the goalie moves to make the block at the post when Player 1 passes to Player 2, who deflects the puck toward the net. The goalie practices this move on both sides.

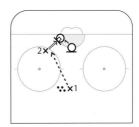

4. In the basic stance at the post, the goalie moves to make the block facing the stick of the player located in front of the net. The goalie practices this move on both sides.

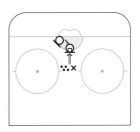

5. In the basic stance at the post, the goalie moves to make the block when Player 1 passes the puck to Player 2. The goalie practices this move on both sides.

Concepts

From a theoretical point of view, the beginner goaltender should be able to understand and apply the following concepts relatively well:

A – Moves
B – Positioning
C – Coverage

Even if most of the training regarding the three concepts mentioned above should mainly be done by intermediate-level goalies (aged 13 to 16 years), it is essential that it be started between the ages of 9 and 12.

This is why the discussion on these three notions will be brief, as skating and the basic techniques continue to be the main focus of on-ice training.

A — Moves

This requires a lot of skating skill on the part of the goalie. Each time there is a pass inside the defensive zone, the goalie must follow the puck as it travels from one opponent to another by pushing off on one leg and stopping using the opposite leg (photos 1 and 2).

Exercises to develop motion

1. Review the skating exercises and moves presented in chapters 1 and 2.

B — *Positioning*

When the puck touches the opponent's stick following the pass, the goalie has to brake and be positioned directly in front of the puck. Therefore, the goalie must have one skate on each side of the imaginary line that links the center of the net to the puck (photos 1 and 2). The goalie is not positioned facing the player (photos 3 and 4).

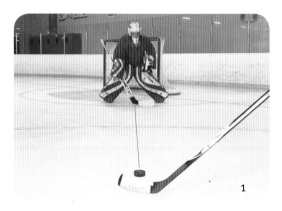

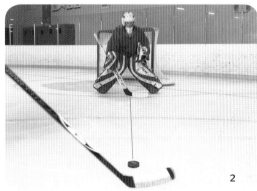

Bad positioning   *Bad positioning*

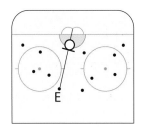

Exercises to develop positioning

1. The coach attaches a rope to the center post of the net. The coach holds the rope above the pucks, which are spread out at different angles. The goalie moves by keeping one skate on each side of the rope.

2. In the basic stance, the goalie has one foot on each side of the rope. The other goalie observes the shooting angles from the height of the puck. The goalie in the net can place both feet to the right or the left of the rope to help the partner view the shooting angles.

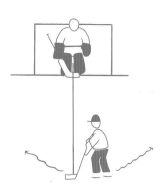

3. The coach attaches a rope to the center post and stretches it to the blade of the goalie's stick. The goalie moves to the left and the right. One skate must be kept on each side of the rope.

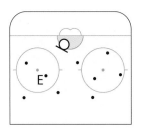

4. The goalie, in the basic stance, takes up the position facing the puck. The coach stands behind the puck and corrects as needed.

C — *Coverage*

Once the beginner goalie understands the concepts behind the moves and positioning, it becomes relatively easy to introduce the idea of covering the space. The more the goalie remains deep inside the goal, the more the goalie offers an opening to the shooter (photo 1).

The more the goalie advances in the direction of the shooter, the more space the goalie covers (photo 2).

Since the maximum amount of space available is in front of the net, the goalie should advance a little farther to cover any opening offered to the player located in front of the net. With respect to the shots coming from a sharper angle, the goalie does not have to advance as far since the available space is already reduced. The goalie's move toward the puck must normally resemble a kind of elongated semi-circle forward motion. These types of moves will allow for maximum coverage of the space, regardless of where the puck originates. Of course, these moves depend on specific criteria:

1

— the goalie's skating skill (the greater the goalie's skill, the farther away he or she can move from the goal);

— the certainty that a shot will be fired at the net (when the goalie is sure of the shot, the goalie can advance a little farther to cover as much of the space as possible. It is more important to understand that any move toward the puck must be executed before the shot is fired. Once the shot is fired, the goalie must remain stationary to maintain maximum stability and balance);

— the possibility that another play will be made at the last second (during a 2-on-1, or a 3-on-2, it is better not to advance toward the player carrying the puck). However, in general, the goalie's heels remain near the semi-circle of the crease*.

2

---

* It is deceiving to think that a beginner goaltender can cover a lot of space, given:
  — the dimensions of the net (the same as those of the NHL);
  — the height of the goalie (between 3.5 and 4.5 feet [1.06 and 1.37 m] on average).

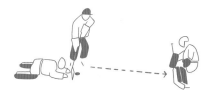

Exercises to develop the ability to cover the space

1. A goalie assumes the basic stance on the goal line, facing the puck. The other goalie observes how the space is covered from the height of the puck.

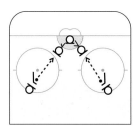

2. The goalie in the net advances more and more toward the puck.

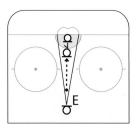

3. Same exercise, but the puck is placed to the right or to the left of the net.

4. The coach attaches a rope to each of the two outside posts of the net. The goalie, in the basic stance, advances toward the puck and realizes that there is less space between the body and the ropes.

5. The other goalie watches how the area is covered from the height of the puck. The coach moves into position to fire a shot. The goalie covers the space, according to the position of the puck. The coach can also shoot on goal. The other goalie watches from the height of the puck.

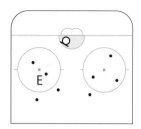

6. The goalie receives the shots coming from extremely wide and narrow angles. The goalie has to realize that he or she does not need to advance as much to meet the shots coming at a narrow angle.

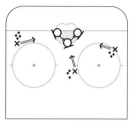

On-ice goalie evaluations

Summary

1. Describe the objectives of evaluating beginner goaltenders.

2. Present a method for running the tests before, during and after the evaluation.

3. Present the tests chosen as well as the procedures required to apply each one.

4. Briefly describe some of the attributes to look for when selecting beginner goaltenders.

	1	2	3	4
Period	Pre-season	Season	Post-season	Off-season
Month	J-A	S-O-N-D-J-F	M-A	M-J
A On-ice training		3. Three on-ice evaluations 3 times during this period		
B Off-ice training				

valuating a goaltender is a very important part of a coach's job. Unfortunately, almost nothing exists on this topic, so the coach must rely on instinct when selecting goaltenders and assessing their progress throughout the season. This chapter will present some of the tests chosen based on:

1. the attributes a beginner goaltender has to have;
2. ease of use;
3. a minimum amount of equipment.

Without guaranteeing absolute success in evaluating your goaltenders, the tests do offer a scale for comparison. The objectives of evaluating goalies, both on the ice and off, are as follows:

1. to determine how good a goalie is based on physical and technical objectives (selection);
2. to determine the strengths and weaknesses of the goalie (to plan the goalie's training);
3. to observe the goalie's improvement (progress).

How to carry out the tests

When the evaluation tests are administered, it is essential to know how to proceed. Moreover, it is critical that the instructions relating to each test be repeated in a similar manner for each participant and each time that the same test is conducted.

Before running the tests

1. Familiarity with the tests

The coach must become familiar with the way the tests are run. Moreover, the goalies must be able to do the tests several times. Inexperience can prevent goalies from performing at their best.

2. Equipment, surfaces and available time

The proper preparation of the equipment and the surfaces to be used during the tests can help make them more effective and reduce the amount of time normally allocated. It would be inappropriate to conduct all the tests in the same day. A period of 2 to 3 training sessions seems reasonable.

Before the Test

1. Warm-up

Just as the goalie would during a game, the player needs a good warm-up for optimal performance.

2. Demonstration and explanation of the tests

It is important to provide a demonstration of the test supported by clear explanations before beginning.

3. Motivation

Motivation is essential during a physical performance check. Therefore, the coach must ensure that all the goalies are equally encouraged.

After the test

1. Interpreting the results

Once the tests are completed, the coach must interpret the results. To do this, the coach will note the strengths and weaknesses of each goalie in order to begin the final selection, to plan the training sessions or to assess the goalie's progress.

On-ice testing*

The measurements noted during the on-ice evaluation tests are as follows:

A — Agility on the ice

1. *Test objective*
To assess the beginner goalie's agility on the ice.
2. *Required equipment*
  - 1 pencil
  - 1 whistle
  - 1 results sheet
  - 1 stopwatch
3. *Goalie equipment*
The goalie wears all equipment and keeps the stick for the entire test
4. *Procedure*
  - The goalie is in the basic stance.
  - At the start signal, the goalie assumes the
    butterfly stance, simulates freezing a puck on the ice using both gloves, then lays down on the stomach. The goalie then reassumes the basic stance. This sequence represents one cycle. The goalie must correctly perform this cycle five times.
  - The coach stops the stopwatch when the goalie correctly reassumes the initial position.
  - The time is recorded to the nearest second.
  - In the event the test is stopped, it is redone. On the second attempt, the stopwatch is not stopped.

* These tests do not have to undergo all the testing stages to be valid.

87

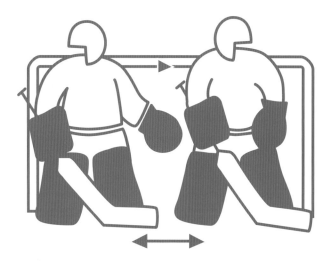

B — Speed of motion between posts

1. *Test objective*
To measure how quickly to goalie moves from one post to the other.
2. *Required equipment*
    — 1 pencil
    — 1 tally sheet
    — 1 stopwatch
    — 1 whistle
3. *Goalie equipment*
    See test A.
4. *Procedure*
    — The goalie is in the basic stance at the goal line. One of his skates must be pressed against one of the posts.
    — At the start signal, the goalie moves while in the basic stance to the other post. Once the goalie reaches the other side, the goalie must press the skate against the post and return to touch the first post. This represents one cycle.
    — The coach stops the stopwatch when the goalie has completed five cycles.
    — The time is recorded to the nearest second.
    — In the event of a fall, or if the test is stopped, it is redone. On the second attempt, the stopwatch is not stopped.

C — Stopping and passing the puck

1. *Test objective*
To assess the beginner goalie's skill in stopping and passing the puck.
2. *Required equipment*
   — 1 pencil
   — 1 tally or results sheet
   — 1 puck
   — 1 stick
3. *Goalie equipment*
   See test A.
4. *Procedure*
   — The goalie is in the basic stance at the top of the crease opposite the neutral zone.
   — The coach shoots the puck along the boards. The goalie performs one or two T-pushes and stops near the boards to stop the puck (see page 56).
   — The goalie then controls the puck and passes it directly to the coach's stick (see page 59).
   — The coach notes the number of times the goalie correctly stops the puck and the number of times he accurately passes the puck.
   — Repeat three times on each side.

T-motion:

Stopping: //

Pass:

Puck: ●

Coach: E

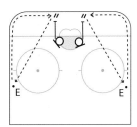

D — Blocking the puck

1. *Test objective*
To assess the goalie's level of skill in blocking a puck.
2. *Required equipment*
   — 1 pencil
   — 1 observation sheet
   — 20 pucks
3. *Goalie equipment*
   See test A.
4. *Procedure*
   — The goalie is in the basic stance, just outside the crease (with heels near the line).
   — The assistant coach is in the slot.
   — The shots are aimed at a precise height in the net, determined in advance.
   The pace must allow the goalie enough time to reassume the basic stance between each shot.

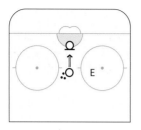

— Therefore, each goalie must receive:

a) 15 low shots to stop using the stick or pads (five pucks in the center, five to the left and five to the right);

b) 15 shots at mid-level to stop using the pads, body, the catching glove or the blocker (five pucks in the center, five to the left and five to the right);

c) 15 high shots to stop using the body, catching glove or the blocker (five pucks in the center, five to the left and five to the right).

— The coach must only note the shots directed at the correct height and at the right time (therefore, a high shot during a series of low shots is not counted).

— The coach must note the number of shots blocked by each goalie at each height. The coach must also observe the style, speed, balance and courage of each goalie. This test, which is both subjective and objective, can nonetheless provide valuable information for the final selection.

Attributes to be observed

It is not always possible, due to a lack of time or help, to test all young goalies both on and off the ice. When this situation arises (or in order to improve the quality of these tests), the coach should observe the following:

A) Is the goalie able to move quickly?

It is very important that a goalie be able to move quickly, since effort is often based on speed. Ensure that the goalie is quick.

B) Does the goalie have a competitive spirit?

It is essential that the goalie feel at ease and be assertive during sporting events, otherwise the player will not be able to handle the tension the player will often be exposed to.

C) Does the goalie listen to advice?

A goalie who does not accept advice will not be able to progress quickly or will always remain at the same level. When it comes to a receptive or an unreceptive goalie, the choice is clear.

D) Is the goalie brave?

A goalie must be courageous to succeed. Indeed, if at each shot, the goalie raises the shoulders, turns the head or retreats into the net, the player will never be able to assume a satisfactory basic stance or be happy in this position.

E) Is the goalie hard-working?

A goalie who has this attribute will work tirelessly to improve the basic moves and to correct the faults that the coach points out. Without a doubt, a hard-working goalie is also disciplined and persistent, which is very important.

F) Is the goalie a good skater?

Since skating is the most important technique in hockey, the goalie must be able to skate relatively well to succeed. A good skater who also likes to mind the net will almost certainly be a good goalie.

G) Does the goalie have good coordination?

The coordination of the eyes, hands and feet is essential to catch or block the pucks aimed at the goalie. If the goalie finds it difficult to catch the balls shot at him or her or to kick the balls easily and accurately, it is almost certain that the job of goalie is not right for that player.

H) Can the goalie easily concentrate?

The goalie must be able to concentrate because during the game, when the puck is near the net, the goalie must be able to focus all attention on the puck and on what the goalie needs to do. Try to notice if the young goalie finds it easy to remain focused while being spoken to and performs instructions quickly and correctly. Does the goalie always stay where the action is during training and games, etc.?

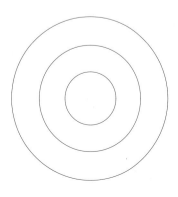

Off-ice
training

ff-ice training is a relatively new training method in North America. Only a small number of coaches used it a few years ago. Given the new training methods developed in other countries around the world, it is easy to see that off-ice training can be a very effective tool for training young players and, in particular, beginner goaltenders. This section will discuss the following:

• off-ice training sessions
• team sports
• individual sports
• off-ice evaluation

To ensure the most complete development possible of young beginner goaltenders, it is important to set specific rules concerning, in particular, the ideal frequency of off-ice training.

	1	2	3	4
Period	Pre-season	Season	Post-season	Off-season
Month	J-A	S-O-N-D-J-F	M-A	M-J
A On-ice training				
B Off-ice training	F*: 4 times/week (90 minutes per session) 2 or 3 team sports 1 or 2 off-ice training sessions	F*: 1 time/week (90 minutes per session) 1 off-ice training session	F*: none	F*: 3–4 times/week (60 minutes per session) 1 or 2 team sports 1 or 2 individual sports

F*: Ideal training frequency to be assigned to off-ice training of the goalie over the course of a hockey season.

Off-ice training sessions

Summary

1. Highlight the importance of off-ice training for the beginner goaltender.

2. List the physical attributes targeted during off-ice training sessions.

3. List the exercises aimed at developing each of the physical attributes listed.

4. Demonstrate a simple method for changing the level of difficulty of these exercises.

5. Explain the periods included in an off-ice training session.

	1	2	3	4
Period	Pre-season	Season	Post-season	Off-season
Month	J-A	S-O-N-D-J-F	M-A	M-J
A On-ice training				
B Off-ice training	1. Off-ice training sessions			

tarting in early July until the end of March (the pre-season and season periods), it is beneficial for the beginner goaltender to have some off-ice training sessions. These sessions, to be repeated once or twice a week during the pre-season period and once a week during the season, must last about 60 minutes. One off-ice training session must consist of general exercises for physical conditioning — whose objective is to increase the beginner goaltender's physical resources — to help promote the following physical attributes:

- speed
- agility
- flexibility
- power
- strength
- endurance
- balance
- coordination

Exercises to promote speed

1. At the coach's signal, run forward, backward, to the right and to the left, for a distance of 5 yards (4.5 m).

2. Rearrange the marker balls according to the different runs. The starting position of the goalie can be standing, lying on his stomach or lying on his back.

3. Run back and forth for 10, 20 or 30 yards (10, 20 or 30 m). These runs can be done running forward, backward or sideways.

4. Sprint around the outside of the markers.

5. Sprint around each marker.

6. Sprint in between the markers.

7. Run around each marker as quickly as possible, then sprint back to the starting point.

a)

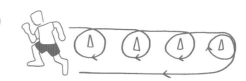

b)

8. At the coach's signal, one of the goalies must try to take possession of the ball from different starting positions.

a)

b)

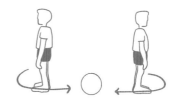

c)

9. Run on the spot as quickly as possible.

10. Run while changing the pace.
For example:

   a) — 10 yards (10 m) at 100% of maximum speed
       — 10 yards (10 m) at 50% of maximum speed
       — 10 yards (10 m) at 100% of maximum speed
       — 10 yards (10 m) at 25% of maximum speed

   b) — 10 yards (10 m) at 25% of maximum speed
       — 30 yards (30 m) at 50% of maximum speed
       — 20 yards (20 m) at 100% of maximum speed
       — 10 yards (10 m) at 25% of maximum speed

11. Run while gradually increasing speed to achieve maximum running speed after 110 yards (100 m).

12. Run back and forth over different distances:
a) 5.5 yards (5 m)
b) 10 yards (10 m)
c) 15 yards (15 m)
d) 20 yards (20 m)
e) 25 yards (25 m)
f) 30 yards (30 m)

13. Jump rope as quickly as possible.

14. Try to touch your partner within a limited space of 10 feet by 10 feet (3 m by 3 m).

15. Run up a steep incline.

16. Walk; at the signal, run 3 yards (3 m), then start walking again.

17. Crouch; at the signal, run 3, 5.5 or 10 yards (3, 5 or 10 m).

18. Walk behind your partner. At the signal, pass your partner at full speed to move in front of your partner. Walk until the next signal.

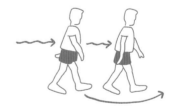

19. Stand; at the signal, bend down and touch the ground as quickly as possible.

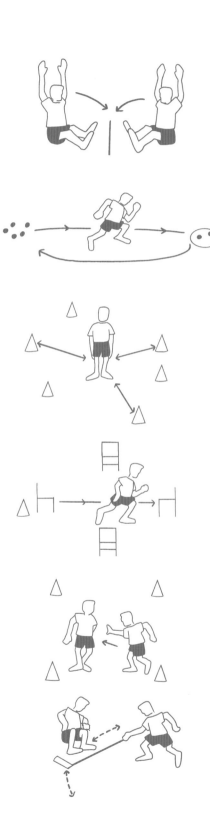

20. Two partners are sitting on the ground, their arms in the air. At the signal, they try to grab the stick lying between them.

21. Run and carry a ball inside a hoop. Return carrying another ball.

22. At the signal, go touch the object the coach has indicated and quickly return to the starting position.

23. At the signal, quickly change seats.

24. One of the two partners tries to avoid being tagged by the other partner inside a limited space.

25. One of the two partners jumps to avoid the stick of the other partner.

Exercises to promote agility

1. Alternately touch each of the pylons several times.

2. Stand, quickly lie down on your stomach, then reassume the initial position.

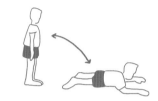

3. Stand, quickly lie down on your back, then reassume the initial position.

4. Run, moving over and under different obstacles. Retrace your steps.

5. Quickly crawl between the legs of a partner. Run 5.5 yards (5 m), then stop to allow your partner to do the same.

6. Play leapfrog.

7. Run and respond to one of the coach's instructions. For example: sit, roll over, walk on all fours, lie on your stomach, lie on your back, crawl on your knees, etc., then stand up and continue running.

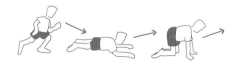

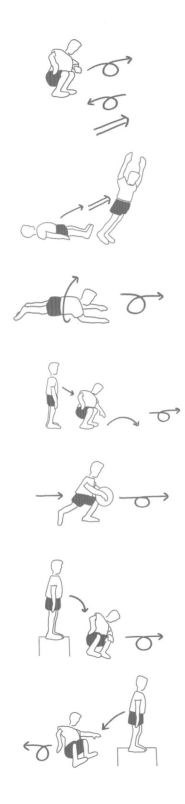

8. Do a forward roll, a backward roll and leap forward.

9. Lie on your back, get up quickly and leap forward.

10. Lie on your stomach, get up quickly and do a forward roll.

11. Stand, crouch as low as possible, leap forward and do a forward roll.

12. Run with the ball in your hands and do a forward roll.

13. Stand on a balance bench, jump to the ground and do a forward roll.

14. Stand on a balance bench, jump backward to the ground and do a backward roll.

15. Jump over a partner crouching on the ground and roll.

16. Quickly run between the markers placed closely together.

17. Stand, quickly touch your right heel and return to the initial position. Repeat on the left.

18. Crouch, sit down, lie down on your stomach, stand up, crouch, etc.

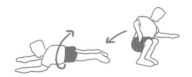

19. Stand, place one knee on the ground, then stand up again.

20. Stand, place both knees on the ground, then stand up again.

Exercises to promote flexibility

Neck

1. Lie on your back and tilt your head forward.

2. Lie on your stomach and tilt your head back.

3. Stand and look to each side as far back on each side as possible.

4. Stand and turn your head.

Shoulders

5. Stand and touch your hands behind your back.

6. Stand, swing your arms back and forth to create large circles.

7. Lean your trunk forward and reach your arms back and up as high as possible.

8. Stand and swing your arms back and forth to make large circles.

9. With the help of a partner, stretch your arms as far back as possible.

Trunk

10. Sit on the ground with arms outstretched and rotate your trunk.

11. Stand with your trunk bent forward and your arms crossed, then rotate your torso.

12. Rest on all fours and do cat stretches.

13. Stand with your left hand on your hip and your right hand behind your head and flex your trunk on the left side. Do the same on the right side. Repeat.

14. Lie on your stomach with your hands behind your head and tilt your trunk backward, release, then lift your hips. Repeat.

15. Work in pairs, bend your trunk forward, then grab each other's shoulders. Apply a downward force to lift your back.

Hips

16. Work in pairs and apply pressure to the back of the person sitting on the ground.

17. Work in pairs and lie on the ground holding each other's hands, then move your legs from one side to the other.

18. Stand, arms outstretched, and move the left foot to the right hand.

19. Crouch, with both hands on the ground, and make a big circle with one leg.

20. Crouch, with both hands on the ground, and alternately stretch one leg on each side.

21. Sit with the soles of your feet together and lower your knees to the ground.

22. Work in pairs and have your partner hold one foot while you touch the ground with your hands.

Legs

23. Crouch, then straighten your legs and stand up, keeping your hands on the ground.

24. Stand, slowly spread your legs apart and return to the starting position.

25. Sit on the ground and turn your head toward your knees.

26. With one knee on the ground, the other leg extended, bend your trunk forward to touch your feet with your hands.

27. Lie on your back and bring one leg toward your trunk using your hands.

28. With both hands on the ground, do the splits.

29. Stand and rotate your knees.

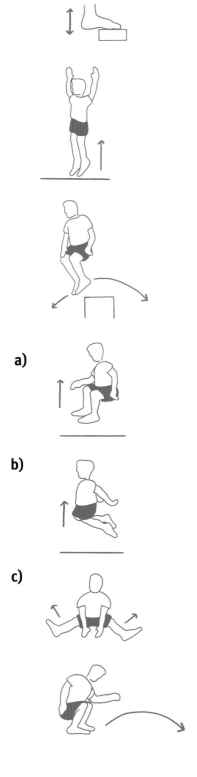

30. Stand with the soles of your feet on a wooden block and raise and lower your heels.

Exercises to promote power

1. Jump as high as possible.

2. Jump over a balance bench with your feet together.

3. Jump as high as possible by performing several moves:
a) with your knees up
b) with your heels and arms back
c) with your legs to each side

a)

b)

c)

4. Crouch, leap as far as possible and land in a crouch.

5. Leap onto a raised bench. Jump backward. As soon as your feet touch the ground, leap back onto the bench.

6. Jump up and perform a one-quarter, a one-half, and a complete turn.

7. Jump on one leg.

8. Jump with your feet together.

9. Take long strides while running.

10. Crouch, with your hands touching the ground, then jump as high as possible.

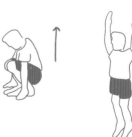

11. Crouch while holding a ball, then leap by throwing the ball as high as possible.

12. Russian dance. Crouch, extend the right leg to one side, then the left.

13. Push your partner who voluntarily resists.

14. Perform a quick 5.5 yard (5 m) run with a long jump at the end.

15. Hop with your feet together, like a slalom skier.

16. Jump three steps at a time with your feet together.

17. Jump over hurdles with your feet together.

18. Leap in different directions.

19. Stand with one foot in front of the other. While jumping, switch the foot that is in front.

20. Throw a medicine ball as hard as possible using both hands.

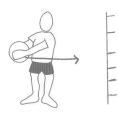

21. Throw a medicine ball as hard as possible on the ground.

22. Throw a medicine ball as hard as possible against a wall.

23. Work in pairs and kick the ball as hard as possible using both feet.

Exercises to promote strength

1. Perform push-ups with your trunk facing the floor.

2. Perform push-ups with your back facing the floor.

3. Perform sit-ups.

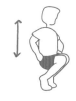

4. Perform knee bends.

5. Carry a partner on your back.

6. Work in pairs and play wheelbarrow.

7. Carry a 15 to 20 pound (7 to 9 kg) weight while running a distance of 20 to 30 yards (20 to 30 m).

8. Play tug-of-war.

9. Climb a rope.

10. Work in pairs and perform upward knee bends.

11. In the push-up position, perform one rotation on one hand and one foot.

12. Work in pairs and pull a hockey stick toward each other.

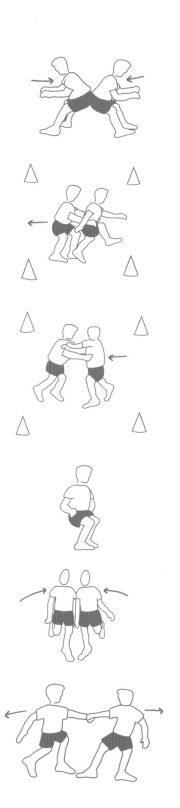

13. Back to back, push your partner.

14. Hold your partner who tries to escape from a limited space.

15. Try to push your partner outside the limited space.

16. Squat as if sitting and remain in this position.

17. Jump on one leg and push your partner using your shoulder.

18. Pull your partner by the arm.

19. Push against a wall.

20. Hold the medicine ball between your feet and move it:
   a) from left to right
   b) up and down
   c) back and forth

a)

b)

c)

21. Grab a ball from your partner's hands.

22. Lift and lower your partner.

23. Extend your back backward.

24. Throw the medicine ball as high as possible.

25. It is also possible to create a circuit:
   — perform 10 exercises stimulating different parts of the body
   — quickly repeat for 30 seconds
   — rest for 30 seconds
   — move on to the next exercise

Exercises to promote endurance

1. Run on the spot. Lift your knees up high for three to five minutes

2. Run for 5 to 10 minutes. Your heart rate must be around 140 beats/minute.

3. Quickly run for 20 to 30 seconds. Rest for 40 to 60 seconds. Repeat several times.

4. Quickly walk over rough terrain.

5. Play one-on-one soccer in a gym.

6. Perform any other exercise requiring significant movement for a prolonged period of time. Exercises focusing on speed and agility are an excellent choice.

Exercises to promote balance

1. Stand, lift one leg to the side and make large circles.

2. Stand and lift one leg in front of you. Close your eyes and swing your arms back and forth.

3. Stand and lower yourself forward to touch the ground with your hands, with one leg stretched straight out behind you. Assume a plank pose and return to the initial position.

a)

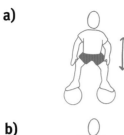

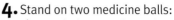

4. Stand on two medicine balls:
   a) crouch down and stand up
   b) simulate the moves used to stop the puck
      with your hands.

b)

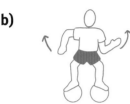

5. Stand on a medicine ball:
   a) place one foot or both feet on the ball
   b) crouch down and stand up
   c) turn around in a circle

a)

b)

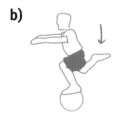

c)

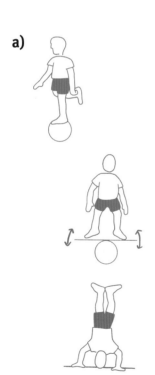

6. Stand, with both feet on a board placed on the medicine ball.

7. Hold your balance while doing a head stand.

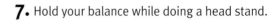

8. Move from a crouching position to standing on the tips of your toes while swinging your arms back and forth. Return to the initial position.

9. Jump on one foot on the marks indicated on the ground. When you land on a mark, keep your balance for three seconds before jumping to another spot.

10. Stand with your arms outstretched and touch your right hand with your left foot while keeping your eyes shut.

11. Sit on the ground and make a pedaling motion with your feet. Only your buttocks should touch the ground.

12. Stand, with one leg stretched out in front of you, crouch and return to the initial position.

13. Stand on the tips of your toes and swing one leg back and forth:
a) with your eyes open
b) with your eyes closed

14. Stand, place one foot against the knee of your other leg, with your hands on your hips with:
a) your eyes open
b) your eyes closed

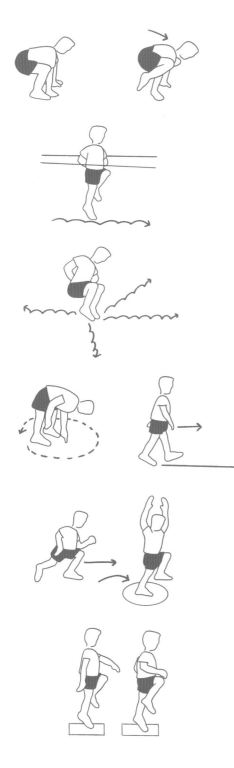

15. Crouch with both hands on the ground. Move forward, rest your knees on your elbows and lift your feet off the ground.

16. Stand on one foot with your hands behind your back and jump between two ropes without touching them.

17. Crouch with your hands behind your back and perform three small jumps forward. Remain stationary for three seconds, then do:
a) three jumps backward
b) three jumps to the right
c) three jumps to the left

18. Stand, place one finger on the ground and quickly walk around your finger five times. Stand up, wait three seconds, then walk in a straight line.

19. Run and jump on one foot inside a hoop. Maintain your balance for five seconds with both arms in the air.

20. Stand with one foot on an 8 x 4 inch (20 x 10 cm) wooden block and skip up and down on the block.

21. Stand on a wooden block, jump and perform a one-quarter, a one-half, and a complete turn:
a) with both feet on the block
b) with one foot on the block

22. Stand with one foot on the wooden block and lean forward to pick up a ball.

23. Walk along an upside-down balance bench or along a low beam:
— forward
— backward
— sideways
— on tiptoe
— crouching
— running
— with a bag of sand on your head
— with a bag of sand on the back of each hand, with arms stretched out to each side
— while dribbling a ball on the ground
— while catching balls thrown at you
— while juggling two balls
— while tossing balls with a partner
— while jumping over the medicine balls placed on the bench

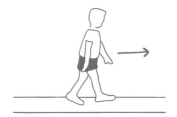

Exercises to promote coordination

1. Run and kick objects scattered on the ground.

2. Stand with your arms stretched out in front of you, drop a ball and catch it before it touches the ground.

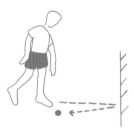

3. Continously kick a ball against the wall.

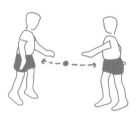

4. Work in pairs and quickly toss a ball:
  — directly
  — with one bounce on the ground
  — from a distance
  — from close up
  — while advancing and retreating
  — while turning around each time

5. Dribble a ball:
  — with one hand
  — while switching hands after each dribble
  — while standing
  — while crouching
  — while kneeling
  — while walking
  — forward
  — backward
  — while running
  — using two balls

6. Continuously throw a ball against a wall as quickly as possible:
— directly
— with one bounce on the ground
— while throwing with one hand and catching with the other
— while catching with both hands

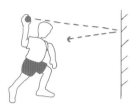

7. Work in pairs and continuously throw a ball against a wall as quickly as possible.

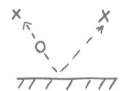

8. Dribble a basketball while looking ahead:
— while walking
— while running
— while turning around
— while zigzagging

9. Work in pairs, with one player dribbling the ball while the other tries to take it away.

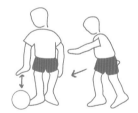

10. Throw a ball near a target on a wall:
— aim higher than the target
— aim to the right of the target
— aim to the left of the target
— aim lower than the target
— aim at the middle of the target

11. Throw balls or bags of sand into hoops of different sizes, placed at various distances.

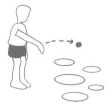

12. Run and jump when you come to a specific spot.

13. Throw a ball at target placed at different heights.

14. Kick a ball at target placed at different heights.

15. Work in pairs and run in all directions while tossing a ball to each other.

16. Dribble a soccer ball in different ways using your feet.

17. Throw a ball in the air. Perform a complete turn and catch the ball.

The Hockey Goalie's Complete Guide

124

18. Hold the ball with your arm outstretched, at shoulder height. Quickly turn around and catch the ball before it touches the ground.

19. Using a tennis racket or a baseball bat, hit a ball thrown:
— from various distances
— at various speeds
— at various heights

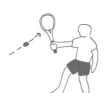

You can also hit the ball using:
— your hands
— your feet

You can also:
— trap the ball
— catch the ball

20. Two goalies stand facing a wall. The coach throws a ball against the wall and names the goalie who must quickly grab the ball.

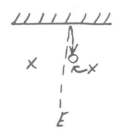

It should be noted that the physical attributes and related exercises are not presented in any particular order. Each physical attribute described is important and must be developed according to the beginner goalie's potential. It is also possible to change the level of difficulty of these exercises. The coach's personality and creativity are important.

For example :
Let's take Exercise 4 for balance:
• stand on two medicine balls

and Exercise 5 for coordination:
• dribble a ball

By combining these two exercises, a new one is created:
   • stand on two medicine balls, dribble the ball

In this way, the young goalie's balance and coordination are developed. Here is another example:

   Let's take Exercice 4 for agility:
   • while running, move over or under different obstacles

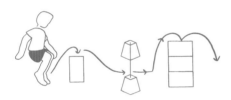

and Exercise 15 for power:
• hop with your feet together, like a slalom skier

By combining these two exercises, a new exercise is created:

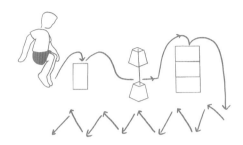

- while running, move over or under different obstacles. Return to the starting point by moving with your feet together, like a skier. The goalie's agility and power are both developed. As you can see from the two previous examples, the coach can modify the level of difficulty of these exercises to promote one or more physical attributes at the same time.

This series of exercises helps you:
— maintain the goalie's interest
— adapt the exercises depending on the goalie's potential
— progress with the goalie, if you have the opportunity to train the goalie for more than one season

The sequence for an off-ice training session

An off-ice training session consists of three precise periods:
1. warm-up
2. development
3. cool-down

1. The warm-up period consists of rotating exercises (neck, shoulders, trunk, hips, knees, ankles), stretching (back, legs, groin, calves), jumps (on one foot, on two feet, on the spot, moving, etc.), running on the spot or moving.

2. The development period of the different physical attributes consists of exercises for general physical development.
   This period can have:
- exercises that focus on one physical attribute
- exercises that focus on two or three physical attributes
- exercises that focus on several physical attributes

The coach can choose which combination to use.

3. The cool-down period consists of group games, walking and relaxation exercises.

5

Team sports

Summary

1. Explain the importance of playing team sports during the pre-season and off-season periods.

2. List the team sports that are the most instructive.

	1	2	3	4
Period	Pre-season	Season	Post-season	Off-season
Month	J-A	S-O-N-D-J-F	M-A	M-J
A **On-ice** **training**				
B **Off-ice** **training**	II. Team sports			II. Team sports

Team sports are extremely useful during the pre- and off-season periods. These sports instill team spirit and a competitive drive, while maintaining the physical fitness of the young goaltender. During these periods, the beginner goaltender must play these team sports once or twice a week, for one to two hours at a time.

Included among the most instructive team sports are:
• soccer
• basketball
• volleyball
• baseball or softball (especially the position of catcher)
• lacrosse
• floor hockey
• field hockey

The hockey coach should strongly encourage the young goalies to play a lot of sports during the pre- and off-season periods, from early May to the end of August.

Individual sports

Summary

1. Explain the importance of playing individual sports during the post-season period.

2. List the best individual sports for this time of the year.

	1	2	3	4
Period	Pre-season	Season	Post-season	Off-season
Month	J-A	S-O-N-D-J-F	M-A	M-J
A On-ice training				
B Off-ice training				III. Individual sports

I ndividual sports have the advantage of being played during the off-season period (even if they are played all year round). Clearly, the goal of the off-season period is to allow the young goaltender to rest and focus on other things, all the while maintaining a certain level of physical fitness.

In order to do this, the young goaltender must play active, individual sports two to three times a week for 60 minutes at a time. Below is a list of the appropriate activities:

- tennis
- squash
- racketball
- table tennis
- skateboarding
- cycling
- gymnastics
- swimming

7 Off-ice goalie evaluations

Summary

1. Explain the importance of off-ice evaluations when choosing beginner goalies.

2. Present the tests chosen as well as the procedures used to apply them.

3. Present an annual tally sheet of off-ice evaluations.

	1	2	3	4
Period	Pre-season	Season	Post-season	Off-season
Month	J-A	S-O-N-D-J-F	M-A	M-J
A **On-ice** **training**				
B **Off-ice** **training**		III. Three off-ice evaluations during this period		

The objectives of off-ice evaluations of beginner goaltenders are the same as those for the on-ice evaluations. Moreover, these tests are applied in much the same way. The advantage of these tests is that they help reveal some of the physical attributes that are essential for any goaltender, making it easier to determine where the greatest physical potential lies. Therefore, a selection can be made based on the long-term development of the goaltenders and not only on the next season. Sometimes, at the start of a season, the beginner goaltender who already has one or two seasons of experience as part of a team will have an advantage over another candidate. However, if it becomes clear, following the off-ice tests, that the other candidate is stronger than the experienced goaltender, this new factor must be included in the selection criteria.

The following measurements are noted during off-ice evaluations:*

- A — General speed
- B — General agility
- C — Muscle strength
- D — Dynamic flexibility
- E — Hip and back flexibility
- F — Hand-eye coordination

---

* These tests are discussed in many manuals on evaluating and are, for the most part, valid and accurate. These tests are taken from the book *L'évaluation en éducation physique* by Rémi Bissonnette, Université de Sherbrooke, 1977, p. 134.

A — Speed

1. *Definition*
An attribute that allows for the rapid execution of one or more moves of the same type within a unit of time.

2. *Required equipment*
- 1 pencil
- 1 results sheet
- 1 or 2 stopwatches
- 1 measuring tape

3. *Goalie equipment*
- running shoes
- shorts
- T-shirt

4. *Procedure*
- The goalie is standing at the starting line. The entire body must be behind the line.
- At the start signal, the goalie runs to the finish line. When the player crosses the finish line, the stopwatch is stopped and the result noted immediately.
- Ensure that the player warmed up properly before this test.
- Two timekeepers are recommended.
- The time is recorded to the nearest second.

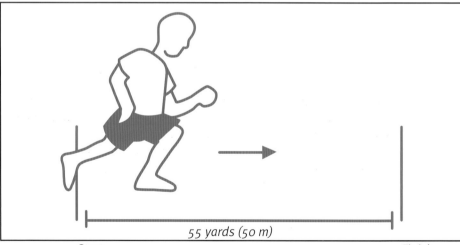

55 yards (50 m)

Start   *Finish*

B — Agility

1. *Definition*

The ability of the body or parts of the body to change direction quickly and accurately.

2. *Required equipment*
- 1 results sheet
- 1 pencil
- 1 measuring tape
- 6 markers
- gymnasium

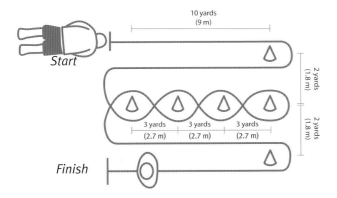

3. *Goalie equipment*

See test A.

4. *Procedure*
- The subject is lying on his stomach. The hands and forehead must be behind the starting line.
- At the signal, the goalie stands up and the stopwatch is started. The player covers the course at full speed. When the finish line is crossed, the stopwatch is stopped. The result is immediately recorded.
- Ensure that the player warmed up properly before the test.
- Two timekeepers are recommended.
- The time is recorded to the nearest second.

C — Muscle strength

1. *Definition*
An ability to demonstrate maximum muscle strength at maximum speed.

2. *Required equipment*
- 1 measuring tape
- 1 results sheet
- 1 pencil
- 1 felt pen
- tape
- A 5-yard (4.5 m) long area

3. *Goalie equipment*
See test A.

4. *Procedure*
- The player is standing behind the starting line, feet slightly apart.
- When the player is ready, the player bends the knees, swings the arms back and forth, then straightens the legs to try to jump as far as possible.
- The player must land on the feet, while trying to avoid falling backward or putting a hand on the ground.
- The coach measures the distance traveled between the starting line and the spot closest to where the player landed (normally the heel).
- The player can try three times and the best result is recorded.
- The distance is calculated to the nearest inch or centimeter.

D — Dynamic flexibililty

1. *Definition*
The ability to quickly repeat bending motions in which the elasticity and stretching of the muscles are important, as well as the recovery time.

2. *Required equipment*
- 1 results sheet
- 1 pencil
- tape (to mark an "X" on the ground and on the wall)
- 1 wall 6 feet (1.8 m) high

3. *Goalie equipment*
See test A.

4. *Procedure*
- The subject is standing with the back to the wall (at 1 foot or 1.5 feet [30 or 45 cm] from the wall), feet shoulder-width apart and his hands in front of the thighs.

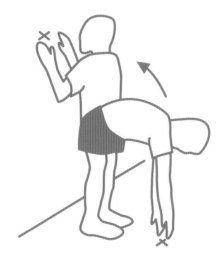

- At the start signal, the player bends the trunk forward, touches the "X" located between the feet with both hands together, stands up, then turns to the left and touches the "X" on the wall. This represents one cycle. The goalie must repeat this cycle as often as possible in 20 seconds.
- The result recorded corresponds to the number of cycles completed in 20 seconds.

E — Hip and back flexibility

1. *Definition*
The range of movement in a joint.

2. *Required equipment*
- 1 results sheet
- 1 pencil
- 1 box
- 1 2 foot (50 cm) ruler

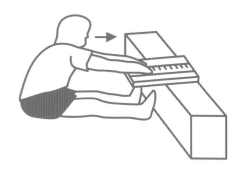

3. *Goalie equipment*
See test A.

4. *Procedure*
- The player sits on the ground and places the feet against the box.
- The player stretches the arms forward and tries to reach as far as possible on the ruler placed on top of the box, while keeping the legs extended forward on the ground. The player must hold the position on the ruler for at least two seconds.
- Ensure that the player has warmed up properly (especially along the backs of the thighs) before this test.
- The result is recorded to the nearest inch or centimeter.

F — Hand-eye coordination

1. *Definition*
The ability to throw and catch objects.

2. *Required equipment*
- 1 results sheet
- 1 pencil
- 1 stopwatch
- tape
- 1 wall and 20 feet (6 m) of open space
- 1 medium-sized rubber ball (similar to a red, white and blue ball)

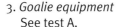

11.5 feet
(3.5 m)

3. *Goalie equipment*
See test A.

4. *Procedure*
- The player stands behind the boundary line.
- At the start signal, the player must throw the ball against the wall, catch it and throw it again as quickly as possible for 30 seconds.
- The result is recorded to the nearest number of catches.
- If the ball goes right past the player or is too far away, the test is done again. During the second attempt, the goalie must get the ball, return to stand behind the line and continue the test.

Annual tally sheet
for off-ice evaluation tests.

Team:

Date: 1ˢᵗ Evaluation

Names	Test A	Test B	Test C	Test D	Test E	Test F
1 —						
2 —						
3 —						
4 —						
5 —						
6 —						

Date: 2ⁿᵈ Evaluation

Names	Test A	Test B	Test C	Test D	Test E	Test F
1 —						
2 —						
3 —						
4 —						
5 —						
6 —						

Date: 3ʳᵈ Evaluation

Names	Test A	Test B	Test C	Test D	Test E	Test F
1 —						
2 —						
3 —						
4 —						
5 —						
6 —						

Off-ice goalie evaluations

3

SECTION

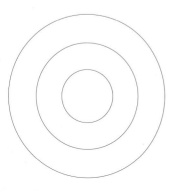

How to coach a goalie

Observing and communicating with the goaltender

Summary

1. Explain the objectives of observing beginner goaltenders.

2. Explain one type of observation and its corresponding sheet.

3. Describe some of the principles of effective communication between the coach and the goaltender.

4. Present a table that includes the different ways of communicating.

A — Observing the goalie

In general, observing is described as paying attention to certain things.

Given the fact that the coach must pay equal attention to all the players, the coach must observe the goaltenders during training and games to the same degree the coach observes all the other players.

The goal of observation is to get to know the goaltender's,

a) athletic ability (learned and unlearned skills);

b) attitude (reaction when faced with competition, relations with players, coaches, etc.).

General observation

This type of observation is used during games played throughout the season.

Sheets are used to:

- compile information on the origin of the shots, as well as the type of shot used to beat the goalie;
- compile information on the location in the net;
- note observations on game situations that preceded the goals scored against the goalie;
- note the different observations on the game played by the opposing team;
- calculate goalie effectiveness as a percentage;
- calculate the overall assessment of the game;
- indicate the name of the goalie, the date and the teams played.

Example of a Game Observation Sheet

Teams: _____ against _____

Date: _____ Goalie: _____

Shots*:

Direct shots: DS

Rebound shots: R

Deflected shots: D

Deke shots: Dk

* Indicate the origin of the goal using the corresponding letter

* Indicate where the goal was scored using the corresponding letter

Observation about each goal scored:

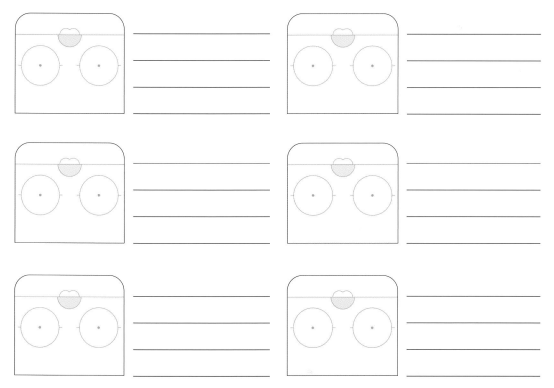

Game Observation Sheet

Teams: _____ against _____

Date: _____ Goalie: _____

Shots*:

Direct shots: DS

Rebound shots: R

Deflected shots: D

Deke shots: Dk

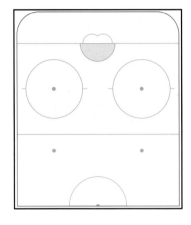

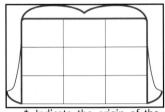

* Indicate the origin of the goal using the corresponding letter

* Indicate where the goal was scored using the corresponding letter

Observation about each goal scored:

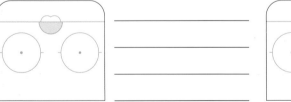

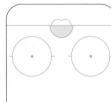

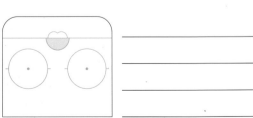

Calculation of the Save Percentage *

Number of shots against	Number of goals against							
	0	1	2	3	4	5	6	7
50	1.000	0.980	0.960	0.940	0.920	0.900	0.880	0.860
49	1.000	0.980	0.959	0.939	0.918	0.898	0.878	0.857
48	1.000	0.979	0.958	0.938	0.917	0.896	0.875	0.854
47	1.000	0.979	0.957	0.936	0.915	0.894	0.872	0.851
46	1.000	0.978	0.957	0.935	0.913	0.891	0.870	0.848
45	1.000	0.978	0.956	0.933	0.911	0.889	0.867	0.844
44	1.000	0.977	0.955	0.932	0.909	0.886	0.864	0.841
43	1.000	0.977	0.953	0.930	0.907	0.884	0.860	0.837
42	1.000	0.976	0.952	0.929	0.905	0.881	0.857	0.833
41	1.000	0.976	0.951	0.927	0.902	0.878	0.854	0.829
40	1.000	0.975	0.950	0.925	0.900	0.875	0.850	0.825
39	1.000	0.974	0.949	0.923	0.897	0.872	0.846	0.821
38	1.000	0.974	0.947	0.921	0.895	0.868	0.842	0.816
37	1.000	0.973	0.946	0.919	0.892	0.865	0.838	0.811
36	1.000	0.972	0.944	0.917	0.889	0.861	0.833	0.806
35	1.000	0.971	0.943	0.914	0.886	0.857	0.829	0.800
34	1.000	0.971	0.941	0.912	0.882	0.853	0.824	0.794
33	1.000	0.970	0.939	0.909	0.879	0.848	0.818	0.788
32	1.000	0.969	0.938	0.906	0.875	0.844	0.813	0.781
31	1.000	0.968	0.935	0.903	0.871	0.839	0.806	0.774
30	1.000	0.967	0.933	0.900	0.867	0.833	0.800	0.767
29	1.000	0.966	0.931	0.897	0.862	0.828	0.793	0.759
28	1.000	0.964	0.929	0.893	0.857	0.821	0.786	0.750
27	1.000	0.963	0.926	0.889	0.852	0.815	0.778	0.741
26	1.000	0.962	0.923	0.885	0.846	0.808	0.769	0.731
25	1.000	0.960	0.920	0.880	0.840	0.800	0.760	0.720
24	1.000	0.958	0.917	0.875	0.833	0.792	0.750	0.708
23	1.000	0.957	0.913	0.870	0.826	0.783	0.739	0.696
22	1.000	0.955	0.909	0.864	0.818	0.773	0.727	0.682
21	1.000	0.952	0.905	0.857	0.810	0.762	0.714	0.667
20	1.000	0.950	0.900	0.850	0.800	0.750	0.700	0.650
19	1.000	0.947	0.895	0.842	0.789	0.737	0.684	0.632
18	1.000	0.944	0.889	0.833	0.778	0.722	0.667	0.611
17	1.000	0.941	0.882	0.824	0.765	0.706	0.647	0.588
16	1.000	0.938	0.875	0.813	0.750	0.688	0.625	0.563
15	1.000	0.933	0.867	0.800	0.733	0.667	0.600	0.533
14	1.000	0.929	0.857	0.786	0.714	0.643	0.571	0.500
13	1.000	0.923	0.846	0.769	0.692	0.615	0.538	0.462
12	1.000	0.917	0.833	0.750	0.667	0.583	0.500	0.417
11	1.000	0.909	0.818	0.727	0.636	0.545	0.455	0.364
10	1.000	0.900	0.800	0.700	0.600	0.500	0.400	0.300
	Save Percentage							

* A save percentage greater than 0.900 is a sign of a good game.

Overall assessment of the game**

Goals against	Period Played		
	1	2	3
0	6	9	12
1	4	6	8
2	0	2	4
3	-2	-1	0
4	-4	-3	-2
5	-7	-5	-4
6	-10	-7	-6
7	-14	-10	-8
8	-18	-13	-10
9	-20	-16	-12
10	-22	-18	-14
Total 1			

Saves	Points
-41	6
36–40	5
31–35	4
26–30	3
21–25	2
16–20	1
–15	0
Total 2	

Overall assessment of the game
Total 1 + Total 2 =

** A total greater than 4 is a sign of a good game.

B — Communicating with goalies

Communication is defined as the transfer of information from one person (the coach) to another (the goalie). Therefore, effective communication between the coach and the goalie is extremely important. Even if the coach is perfectly aware of the goalies' weaknesses (as well as possible solutions), the coach will never be able to help them improve if the coach cannot communicate adequately with them. To communicate with beginner goaltenders, a few basic principles have to be followed:

1. Ensure that your language can be understood by a child aged 8 to 12.
   It does not help to explain a technique using big words if most of the words are meaningless to a young goaltender. Try instead to use simple, imaginative and precise language.
2. Always point out the connections between the new ideas that you are proposing and the old ideas that they are already familiar with, which will indicate to young goaltenders that the lessons will progress over the course of the season.
3. Maintain a particular verbal flow depending on the complexity and the novelty of the message. If the topic raised is easy and familiar to the goalie, a rapid pace of communicating (verbal flow) can be used. On the other hand, if the topic is being raised for the first time or is relatively complex, use a slower verbal pace.
4. Repeat the message as often as necessary in different ways and by varying it.

The coach must repeat the message to ensure the young goaltender understands. Repetition is essential for the message to be understood well.
A good way of checking to see if the message was completely understood by the young goaltender is to make the goalie repeat, in the goalie's own words, everything the coach just explained.

The following diagram shows successful communication between the coach and the goalie.

Diagram showing the successful transmission of a message between the coach and goalie

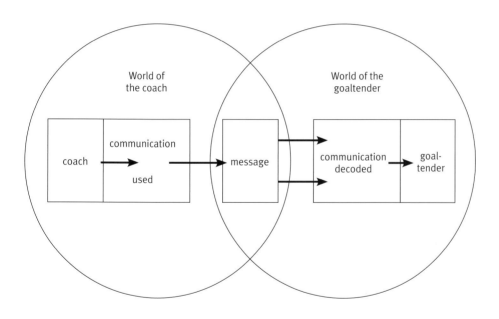

Diagram I: The message is part of the coach's world and the goalie's world. Therefore, the message follows the previously mentioned principles. Communication is successful.

If, on the other hand, the communication used does not follow or use one or several of the criteria previously mentioned, it is highly unlikely that the message will ever be understood by the goalie.

Diagram of inadequate communication

World of
the coach

World of the
goaltender

| coach | communication |
| | used |

message

goal-
tender

Diagram II: The message does not follow some of the principles of communication and cannot penetrate the world of the goalie. Therefore, the communication is inadequate.

Means of communication

The coach has a wide variety of means of communicating. The satisfactory choice of one or several of these means usually allows for productive communication between the coach and the goaltender.

Types of communication

1. Verbal communication

A verbal exchange between the coach and the goaltender.

2. Graphic communication

The use of a diagram to explain a game situation

3. Visual communication

Photos taken from books, newspapers, hockey cards, drawings, etc.

4. Written communication

A written description of a technical move, point by point.

Example:
1. The full length of the pad is touching the ice.
2. The trunk is upright and the buttocks are raised to cover as much area as possible in the top of the net. The goalie's head is held high to watch the play unfold.
3. The gloves are placed on each side of the body.
4. The stick is placed directly in front.
5. The weight of the body is placed over the knees.

5. Statistical communication

Statistics drawn from the game observation sheets.

Examples:
- number of goals granted during the game
- number of shots/number of goals
- number of shots/number of rebounds
- number of goals in the upper, middle and lower levels of the net/number of shots in the upper, middle and lower levels of the net

6. Audio-visual communication

Audio-visual recordings of the training sessions or the games.

7. Multiple communication means

The simultaneous use of two, three or four means of communication.

Correcting beginner goaltenders

Summary

1. Present a useful pedagogical progression when correcting beginner goaltenders.

2. Describe some of the important points to highlight when correcting beginner goaltenders.

The coach, in addition to offering learning exercises concentrating on skating techniques (chapter 1) and on basic techniques (chapter 2), must sometimes correct the team's goaltenders. Normally, specific corrective exercises should never take place at the beginning of the season. It is preferable to observe the goaltenders during training camp and the first few months of the regular season.* This is perfectly normal. How can you correct a goaltender if you do not know the player's strengths and his weaknesses? Many coaches think that it is more difficult to correct a goaltender than a forward. Fortunately, this myth seems to be fading. In fact, correcting a goalie simply requires that some teaching steps be followed.

---

* The chapter dealing with observing and communicating with goaltenders explains some of the methods of observation (see chapter 8).

Suggested pedagogical progression

Step 1

The coach must create a climate of trust with the goalie. Therefore, the corrections must not be made haphazardly. The coach must show the goalie (using proof supported by written notes or observations) that the goalie suffers from a real and consistent weakness. The goalie must be made aware of the problem before beginning the corrective exercises.

Example for step 1

The coach points out to the goalie that, during previous games, there were eight opportunities to move when there was a pass from the corner to the crease and that none of these opportunities was taken or successful. The observation sheets for the previous games indicate this.

Step 2

The coach must explain the technical move using different means of communication (see chapter 8). This step is absolutely necessary if the goalie is to become mentally aware of the mechanics of the move.

Examples for step 2

1. *The coach shows the photo of a push-off performed by the goalie.*
2. *The important technical points are noted.*
3. *A diagram of the situation helps to describe the direction of the push-off.*

Step 3

The coach must create one or two specific, corrective exercises. These exercises will help to show the goaltender the right move to make in contrast to the error pointed out. These exercises must be repeated several times. The repetitions will allow for the goalie to become physically aware of the mechanics of the move and for the goalie to become familiar with this particular move.

Examples for step 3

The coach creates a few specific corrective exercises.

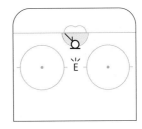

At the coach's signal, the goalie moves from the post to the crease.

Step 4

The coach must create a game situation (as real as possible) where the goalie may be tempted to make the same mistake. This step must be repeated until the goalie has developed new, automatic moves. Otherwise, the new move will be forgotten as soon as a stressful situation arises (e.g., during an important game).

Examples for step 4

The coach creates corrective exercises that resemble actual game situations.

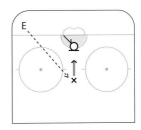

A pass from the corner to the crease for the shot.

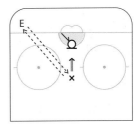

The player in the crease passes to the coach who is in the corner of the rink. When the coach receives the puck, the coach moves into the crease to make the shot.

A few important points to remember when creating corrective exercises

- Correct only one or two problems at a time.
- Respect the goalie's rate of learning and do not jump too quickly from one pedagogical step to another. Be patient and this will pay off in the long run.
- The percentage of corrective exercises must not exceed 10 to 15% of the total time devoted to on-ice training. The rest of the time should be spent on skating exercises, basic techniques, shooting and simulated games.
- The exercise must respect the speed at which the goalie can move. (For example, during passes between two or three players, does the goalie have the time to move accordingly?)
- The exercise must respect the recovery speed of the goalie. (For example, does he have the time to get up before he faces another player?)
- The success rate of the goalie must be roughly 6 to 8 saves on a total of 10 attempts. Otherwise, the corrective exercise is too fast or too complex for the goaltender.
- Be careful when using the corrective exercises; if these are introduced without any preparation on your part or in a negative manner, it is highly unlikely that the goalie will demonstrate a noticeable improvement.
- Never introduce corrective exercises the day before a game. This will have the effect of creating doubt in the mind of the goalie and the goalie's personal preparation will reflect this. Wait instead until the next practice to discuss them.
- The number of pucks that the goalie saves during practice is not a measure of his success.

10

The role of the goalie coach

Summary

1. Present the four types of situations in which the goalie coach must intervene.
2. Briefly describe the roles of the goalie coach during on-ice training.
3. Briefly describe the roles of the goalie coach during off-ice training.
4. Briefly describe the roles of the goalie coach during a game.
5. Briefly describe the administrative tasks of the goalie coach.

Certainly, the head coach cannot train the team's two goalies as well as when there is help by a coach assigned to the goalies. Over the last few years, more and more teams at all levels have been using these specialists. While this effort is laudable, on many occasions, the goalie coach cannot justify this job with the team. This is mostly due to ignorance (on the part of the head coach and the goalie specialist) about the roles that the goalie coach has to play to create a climate that promotes learning. This chapter will list these roles. They are not described in detail because most of them can be adapted in different ways, depending on the category, the coach, the caliber of the game and the goaltenders present.

First of all, the goalie coach plays a role in four types of specific situations:

1. On-ice training
2. Off-ice training
3. Games
4. The goalie coach's own personal preparation

The role of the goalie coach

1. On-ice training

During on-ice training, the goalie coach must:

A — Observe the goaltenders

A coach who wants to propose changes and offer information to the goalies must, above all, be a good observer. Various methods for doing this were described in the chapter on observation (see chapter 8).

B — Communicate with the goaltenders

The coach must be able to communicate the results of the observations to the goalies. This point is very important as it allows the goalies to understand what their weaknesses are in order to correct them. In the chapter on communication, you will find different ways of achieving effective communication (see chapter 8).

C — Periodically evaluate the goaltenders

As in all sports, specific assessments are necessary. To do this, tests concentrating on technique can be conducted at the beginning, in the middle and at the end of the season.

Several tests are described in the chapter on this topic (see chapter 3).

D — Prepare and motivate the goaltenders

The coach must prepare the team's goalies in a positive manner for training and for the games. The coach must also create a climate that promotes the kind of motivation that will help the team's goalies to improve.

E — Create training sessions adapted to the goaltenders

Training sessions must contain exercises concentrating on specific skating techniques, basic techniques and corrective moves.

2. Off-ice training

During off-ice training, the coach must:

A — Prepare the training sessions during the pre-season

Off-ice training during the pre-season must be designed to adequately prepare the goalie for the coming season. For beginner goalies, all of the training consists of general exercises for physical fitness.

B — Prepare training during the season

The objective of off-ice training during the season is to improve or maintain the goalie's general physical fitness. This type of training for beginner goalies does not vary much from pre-season off-ice training (see chapter 4).

C — Periodically evaluate the goaltenders

Off-ice evaluations primarily concentrate on understanding the physical fitness of the beginner goalie. These tests, which can be done at the beginning, in the middle and the end of the season, are described in the chapter on off-ice evaluations (see chapter 7).

3. Games

During the games, the goalie coach must:

A — Select the starting goalie

Given the coach's knowledge of the team's goalies, the coach must decide on the best goalie available for the game. The goalie coach must then communicate this decision to the head coach and to the goalies. Since they are relatively young, they must be given, at all costs, the chance to participate in games as often as possible.

Various methods of substitution can be used for beginner goalies:
- Alternate between games
- Alternate between periods
- Alternate between half periods
- Alternate every two or three line changes
- Alternate after each goal
- Alternate after every two goals

B — Prepare and motivate the substitute beginner goaltender

Before the game, the goalie coach may be called upon to play a role in mentally preparing the goalies.

To achieve this, the goalie coach must discuss the following with the goalie:
- observations about the opposing team
- observations about the opposing players
- a review of the basic techniques
- a review of specific game situations:

- breakaway
- 1-on-1
- 2-on-1
- 3-on-1
- 3-on-2
— player behind the net
— statistics for the last game against this team
— any other topic considered appropriate by the coach

C — Prepare a warm-up before the game

The warm-up is very important because it allows the goaltenders to practice some technical elements that they will have to perform during a game

D — Observe the goaltender during the game

Once the game has started, the goalie coach must remain and observe. Different observation methods are possible. For this topic, please refer to chapter 8.

E — Correct and instruct during the game or between periods

Depending on the type of substitution, the coach can communicate with the goalies during the game or only between periods. To be effective, the coach must have relevant information to communicate.
  Usually, the following information is useful:
  — sheet summarizing the shots on goal
  — players that shot
  — types of shots
  — origin and direction of the shots
  — opposing players that are especially dangerous
  — tactics used by the opposing team
  — technical mistakes
  — good plays made by the goaltender

F — Take responsibility for changes during the game

Sometimes, the goalie coach may be forced to change goalies. This decision is extremely complicated, for a bad decision can lead to a loss or have a negative impact on the goalie being replaced.
  A few questions should be asked before any unplanned substitution:
  — Can the team still win the game?
  — Is the goaltender directly responsible for the goals against the team?
  — Will the goaltender be psychologically affected by staying in the game or by being removed from the game?
  — Can the substitute goaltender adequately replace the goaltender playing?

G — Observe the opposing goaltenders

Because the goalie coach is a resource person in this area, the goalie coach can easily observe the opposing goaltenders during the game and communicate any weaknesses noted to the head coach, who, in turn, will communicate these to the forwards.

4. Personal preparation of the coach

The coach's personal preparation determines, in large part, the quality of the teaching. Therefore, it is very important for the goalie coach to keep some files up to date:

1. A file on training done since the beginning of the season:
— on the ice
— off the ice

2. A file on the observations noted:
— during practice
— during the games

3. A file containing various statistics:
— individual average
— team average
— number of shots, saves, rebounds
— number of goals, the location, the types of shots
— number of wins and losses

4. A file containing the results from the evaluation tests:
— on the ice
— off the ice

Conclusion

The Hockey Goalie's Complete Guide is not intended to be a rigid tool in the hands of coaches, parents and goaltenders, but rather a reference tool that they can consult and adapt according to their specific needs. Reading and applying, even in part, the advice presented in this book will certainly help make the people involved in minor hockey more aware of the importance of developing young goaltenders at the same pace as the other players.

Moreover, it is hoped that this new reference tool will help promote new ideas in an area of hockey that has long been ignored.

Appendix—Work sheets for coaches

Game Observation Sheet

Teams: _____ against _____

Date: _____ Goalie: _____

Shots*:

Direct shot: DS

Rebound shot: R

Deflected shot: D

Deke shot: Dk

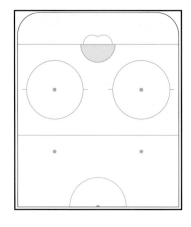

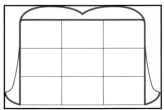

* Indicate the origin of the goal using the corresponding letter

* Indicate where the goal was scored using the corresponding letter

Observation about each goal scored:

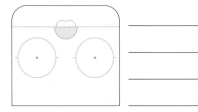
_____
_____
_____

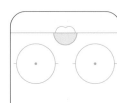

_____
_____

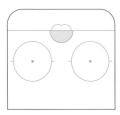
_____
_____
_____

_____
_____

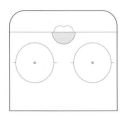
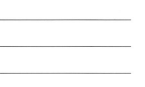
_____
_____

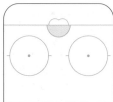
_____
_____
_____

Calculation of the Save Percentage *

		Number of goals against							
		0	1	2	3	4	5	6	7
	50	1.000	0.980	0.960	0.940	0.920	0.900	0.880	0.860
	49	1.000	0.980	0.959	0.939	0.918	0.898	0.878	0.857
	48	1.000	0.979	0.958	0.938	0.917	0.896	0.875	0.854
	47	1.000	0.979	0.957	0.936	0.915	0.894	0.872	0.851
	46	1.000	0.978	0.957	0.935	0.913	0.891	0.870	0.848
	45	1.000	0.978	0.956	0.933	0.911	0.889	0.867	0.844
	44	1.000	0.977	0.955	0.932	0.909	0.886	0.864	0.841
	43	1.000	0.977	0.953	0.930	0.907	0.884	0.860	0.837
	42	1.000	0.976	0.952	0.929	0.905	0.881	0.857	0.833
	41	1.000	0.976	0.951	0.927	0.902	0.878	0.854	0.829
	40	1.000	0.975	0.950	0.925	0.900	0.875	0.850	0.825
	39	1.000	0.974	0.949	0.923	0.897	0.872	0.846	0.821
	38	1.000	0.974	0.947	0.921	0.895	0.868	0.842	0.816
	37	1.000	0.973	0.946	0.919	0.892	0.865	0.838	0.811
	36	1.000	0.972	0.944	0.917	0.889	0.861	0.833	0.806
Number of shots against	35	1.000	0.971	0.943	0.914	0.886	0.857	0.829	0.800
	34	1.000	0.971	0.941	0.912	0.882	0.853	0.824	0.794
	33	1.000	0.970	0.939	0.909	0.879	0.848	0.818	0.788
	32	1.000	0.969	0.938	0.906	0.875	0.844	0.813	0.781
	31	1.000	0.968	0.935	0.903	0.871	0.839	0.806	0.774
	30	1.000	0.967	0.933	0.900	0.867	0.833	0.800	0.767
	29	1.000	0.966	0.931	0.897	0.862	0.828	0.793	0.759
	28	1.000	0.964	0.929	0.893	0.857	0.821	0.786	0.750
	27	1.000	0.963	0.926	0.889	0.852	0.815	0.778	0.741
	26	1.000	0.962	0.923	0.885	0.846	0.808	0.769	0.731
	25	1.000	0.960	0.920	0.880	0.840	0.800	0.760	0.720
	24	1.000	0.958	0.917	0.875	0.833	0.792	0.750	0.708
	23	1.000	0.957	0.913	0.870	0.826	0.783	0.739	0.696
	22	1.000	0.955	0.909	0.864	0.818	0.773	0.727	0.682
	21	1.000	0.952	0.905	0.857	0.810	0.762	0.714	0.667
	20	1.000	0.950	0.900	0.850	0.800	0.750	0.700	0.650
	19	1.000	0.947	0.895	0.842	0.789	0.737	0.684	0.632
	18	1.000	0.944	0.889	0.833	0.778	0.722	0.667	0.611
	17	1.000	0.941	0.882	0.824	0.765	0.706	0.647	0.588
	16	1.000	0.938	0.875	0.813	0.750	0.688	0.625	0.563
	15	1.000	0.933	0.867	0.800	0.733	0.667	0.600	0.533
	14	1.000	0.929	0.857	0.786	0.714	0.643	0.571	0.500
	13	1.000	0.923	0.846	0.769	0.692	0.615	0.538	0.462
	12	1.000	0.917	0.833	0.750	0.667	0.583	0.500	0.417
	11	1.000	0.909	0.818	0.727	0.636	0.545	0.455	0.364
	10	1.000	0.900	0.800	0.700	0.600	0.500	0.400	0.300
		Save Percentage							

* A save percentage greater than 0.900 is a sign of a good game.

Overall assessment of the game**

Goals against	Period Played		
	1	2	3
0	6	9	12
1	4	6	8
2	0	2	4
3	-2	-1	0
4	-4	-3	-2
5	-7	-5	-4
6	-10	-7	-6
7	-14	-10	-8
8	-18	-13	-10
9	-20	-16	-12
10	-22	-18	-14
Total 1			

Saves	Points
-41	6
36–40	5
31–35	4
26–30	3
21–25	2
16–20	1
−15	0
Total 2	

Overall assessment of the game
Total 1 + Total 2 =

** A total greater than 4 is a sign of a good game.

Game Observation Sheet

Teams: _____ against _____

Date: _____ Goalie: _____

Shots*:

Direct shot: DS

Rebound shot: R

Deflected shot: D

Deke shot: Dk

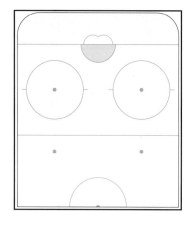

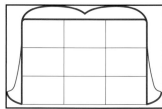

* Indicate where the goal was scored using the corresponding letter

* Indicate the origin of the goal using the corresponding letter

Observation about each goal scored:

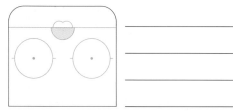 

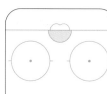

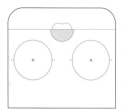 _____

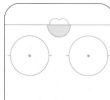 

_____

Calculation of the Save Percentage *

		Number of goals against							
		0	1	2	3	4	5	6	7
Number of shots against	50	1.000	0.980	0.960	0.940	0.920	0.900	0.880	0.860
	49	1.000	0.980	0.959	0.939	0.918	0.898	0.878	0.857
	48	1.000	0.979	0.958	0.938	0.917	0.896	0.875	0.854
	47	1.000	0.979	0.957	0.936	0.915	0.894	0.872	0.851
	46	1.000	0.978	0.957	0.935	0.913	0.891	0.870	0.848
	45	1.000	0.978	0.956	0.933	0.911	0.889	0.867	0.844
	44	1.000	0.977	0.955	0.932	0.909	0.886	0.864	0.841
	43	1.000	0.977	0.953	0.930	0.907	0.884	0.860	0.837
	42	1.000	0.976	0.952	0.929	0.905	0.881	0.857	0.833
	41	1.000	0.976	0.951	0.927	0.902	0.878	0.854	0.829
	40	1.000	0.975	0.950	0.925	0.900	0.875	0.850	0.825
	39	1.000	0.974	0.949	0.923	0.897	0.872	0.846	0.821
	38	1.000	0.974	0.947	0.921	0.895	0.868	0.842	0.816
	37	1.000	0.973	0.946	0.919	0.892	0.865	0.838	0.811
	36	1.000	0.972	0.944	0.917	0.889	0.861	0.833	0.806
	35	1.000	0.971	0.943	0.914	0.886	0.857	0.829	0.800
	34	1.000	0.971	0.941	0.912	0.882	0.853	0.824	0.794
	33	1.000	0.970	0.939	0.909	0.879	0.848	0.818	0.788
	32	1.000	0.969	0.938	0.906	0.875	0.844	0.813	0.781
	31	1.000	0.968	0.935	0.903	0.871	0.839	0.806	0.774
	30	1.000	0.967	0.933	0.900	0.867	0.833	0.800	0.767
	29	1.000	0.966	0.931	0.897	0.862	0.828	0.793	0.759
	28	1.000	0.964	0.929	0.893	0.857	0.821	0.786	0.750
	27	1.000	0.963	0.926	0.889	0.852	0.815	0.778	0.741
	26	1.000	0.962	0.923	0.885	0.846	0.808	0.769	0.731
	25	1.000	0.960	0.920	0.880	0.840	0.800	0.760	0.720
	24	1.000	0.958	0.917	0.875	0.833	0.792	0.750	0.708
	23	1.000	0.957	0.913	0.870	0.826	0.783	0.739	0.696
	22	1.000	0.955	0.909	0.864	0.818	0.773	0.727	0.682
	21	1.000	0.952	0.905	0.857	0.810	0.762	0.714	0.667
	20	1.000	0.950	0.900	0.850	0.800	0.750	0.700	0.650
	19	1.000	0.947	0.895	0.842	0.789	0.737	0.684	0.632
	18	1.000	0.944	0.889	0.833	0.778	0.722	0.667	0.611
	17	1.000	0.941	0.882	0.824	0.765	0.706	0.647	0.588
	16	1.000	0.938	0.875	0.813	0.750	0.688	0.625	0.563
	15	1.000	0.933	0.867	0.800	0.733	0.667	0.600	0.533
	14	1.000	0.929	0.857	0.786	0.714	0.643	0.571	0.500
	13	1.000	0.923	0.846	0.769	0.692	0.615	0.538	0.462
	12	1.000	0.917	0.833	0.750	0.667	0.583	0.500	0.417
	11	1.000	0.909	0.818	0.727	0.636	0.545	0.455	0.364
	10	1.000	0.900	0.800	0.700	0.600	0.500	0.400	0.300
		Save Percentage							

* A save percentage greater than 0.900 is a sign of a good game.

Overall assessment of the game**

Goals against	Period Played		
	1	2	3
0	6	9	12
1	4	6	8
2	0	2	4
3	-2	-1	0
4	-4	-3	-2
5	-7	-5	-4
6	-10	-7	-6
7	-14	-10	-8
8	-18	-13	-10
9	-20	-16	-12
10	-22	-18	-14
Total 1			

Saves	Points
-41	6
36–40	5
31–35	4
26–30	3
21–25	2
16–20	1
–15	0
Total 2	

Overall assessment of the game	
Total 1 + Total 2 =	

** A total greater than 4 is a sign of a good game.

Game Observation Sheet

Teams: _____ against _____

Date: _____ Goalie: _____

Shots*:

Direct shot: DS

Rebound shot: R

Deflected shot: D

Deke shot: Dk

* Indicate where the goal was scored using the corresponding letter

* Indicate the origin of the goal using the corresponding letter

Observation about each goal scored:

_____

_____

_____

_____

_____

_____

_____

_____

_____

_____

_____

_____

_____

_____

_____

_____

_____

_____

Calculation of the Save Percentage *

		Number of goals against						
		0	1	2	3	4	5	6	7

<table>
<tr><th></th><th>0</th><th>1</th><th>2</th><th>3</th><th>4</th><th>5</th><th>6</th><th>7</th></tr>
<tr><td>50</td><td>1.000</td><td>0.980</td><td>0.960</td><td>0.940</td><td>0.920</td><td>0.900</td><td>0.880</td><td>0.860</td></tr>
<tr><td>49</td><td>1.000</td><td>0.980</td><td>0.959</td><td>0.939</td><td>0.918</td><td>0.898</td><td>0.878</td><td>0.857</td></tr>
<tr><td>48</td><td>1.000</td><td>0.979</td><td>0.958</td><td>0.938</td><td>0.917</td><td>0.896</td><td>0.875</td><td>0.854</td></tr>
<tr><td>47</td><td>1.000</td><td>0.979</td><td>0.957</td><td>0.936</td><td>0.915</td><td>0.894</td><td>0.872</td><td>0.851</td></tr>
<tr><td>46</td><td>1.000</td><td>0.978</td><td>0.957</td><td>0.935</td><td>0.913</td><td>0.891</td><td>0.870</td><td>0.848</td></tr>
<tr><td>45</td><td>1.000</td><td>0.978</td><td>0.956</td><td>0.933</td><td>0.911</td><td>0.889</td><td>0.867</td><td>0.844</td></tr>
<tr><td>44</td><td>1.000</td><td>0.977</td><td>0.955</td><td>0.932</td><td>0.909</td><td>0.886</td><td>0.864</td><td>0.841</td></tr>
<tr><td>43</td><td>1.000</td><td>0.977</td><td>0.953</td><td>0.930</td><td>0.907</td><td>0.884</td><td>0.860</td><td>0.837</td></tr>
<tr><td>42</td><td>1.000</td><td>0.976</td><td>0.952</td><td>0.929</td><td>0.905</td><td>0.881</td><td>0.857</td><td>0.833</td></tr>
<tr><td>41</td><td>1.000</td><td>0.976</td><td>0.951</td><td>0.927</td><td>0.902</td><td>0.878</td><td>0.854</td><td>0.829</td></tr>
<tr><td>40</td><td>1.000</td><td>0.975</td><td>0.950</td><td>0.925</td><td>0.900</td><td>0.875</td><td>0.850</td><td>0.825</td></tr>
<tr><td>39</td><td>1.000</td><td>0.974</td><td>0.949</td><td>0.923</td><td>0.897</td><td>0.872</td><td>0.846</td><td>0.821</td></tr>
<tr><td>38</td><td>1.000</td><td>0.974</td><td>0.947</td><td>0.921</td><td>0.895</td><td>0.868</td><td>0.842</td><td>0.816</td></tr>
<tr><td>37</td><td>1.000</td><td>0.973</td><td>0.946</td><td>0.919</td><td>0.892</td><td>0.865</td><td>0.838</td><td>0.811</td></tr>
<tr><td>36</td><td>1.000</td><td>0.972</td><td>0.944</td><td>0.917</td><td>0.889</td><td>0.861</td><td>0.833</td><td>0.806</td></tr>
<tr><td>35</td><td>1.000</td><td>0.971</td><td>0.943</td><td>0.914</td><td>0.886</td><td>0.857</td><td>0.829</td><td>0.800</td></tr>
<tr><td>34</td><td>1.000</td><td>0.971</td><td>0.941</td><td>0.912</td><td>0.882</td><td>0.853</td><td>0.824</td><td>0.794</td></tr>
<tr><td>33</td><td>1.000</td><td>0.970</td><td>0.939</td><td>0.909</td><td>0.879</td><td>0.848</td><td>0.818</td><td>0.788</td></tr>
<tr><td>32</td><td>1.000</td><td>0.969</td><td>0.938</td><td>0.906</td><td>0.875</td><td>0.844</td><td>0.813</td><td>0.781</td></tr>
<tr><td>31</td><td>1.000</td><td>0.968</td><td>0.935</td><td>0.903</td><td>0.871</td><td>0.839</td><td>0.806</td><td>0.774</td></tr>
<tr><td>30</td><td>1.000</td><td>0.967</td><td>0.933</td><td>0.900</td><td>0.867</td><td>0.833</td><td>0.800</td><td>0.767</td></tr>
<tr><td>29</td><td>1.000</td><td>0.966</td><td>0.931</td><td>0.897</td><td>0.862</td><td>0.828</td><td>0.793</td><td>0.759</td></tr>
<tr><td>28</td><td>1.000</td><td>0.964</td><td>0.929</td><td>0.893</td><td>0.857</td><td>0.821</td><td>0.786</td><td>0.750</td></tr>
<tr><td>27</td><td>1.000</td><td>0.963</td><td>0.926</td><td>0.889</td><td>0.852</td><td>0.815</td><td>0.778</td><td>0.741</td></tr>
<tr><td>26</td><td>1.000</td><td>0.962</td><td>0.923</td><td>0.885</td><td>0.846</td><td>0.808</td><td>0.769</td><td>0.731</td></tr>
<tr><td>25</td><td>1.000</td><td>0.960</td><td>0.920</td><td>0.880</td><td>0.840</td><td>0.800</td><td>0.760</td><td>0.720</td></tr>
<tr><td>24</td><td>1.000</td><td>0.958</td><td>0.917</td><td>0.875</td><td>0.833</td><td>0.792</td><td>0.750</td><td>0.708</td></tr>
<tr><td>23</td><td>1.000</td><td>0.957</td><td>0.913</td><td>0.870</td><td>0.826</td><td>0.783</td><td>0.739</td><td>0.696</td></tr>
<tr><td>22</td><td>1.000</td><td>0.955</td><td>0.909</td><td>0.864</td><td>0.818</td><td>0.773</td><td>0.727</td><td>0.682</td></tr>
<tr><td>21</td><td>1.000</td><td>0.952</td><td>0.905</td><td>0.857</td><td>0.810</td><td>0.762</td><td>0.714</td><td>0.667</td></tr>
<tr><td>20</td><td>1.000</td><td>0.950</td><td>0.900</td><td>0.850</td><td>0.800</td><td>0.750</td><td>0.700</td><td>0.650</td></tr>
<tr><td>19</td><td>1.000</td><td>0.947</td><td>0.895</td><td>0.842</td><td>0.789</td><td>0.737</td><td>0.684</td><td>0.632</td></tr>
<tr><td>18</td><td>1.000</td><td>0.944</td><td>0.889</td><td>0.833</td><td>0.778</td><td>0.722</td><td>0.667</td><td>0.611</td></tr>
<tr><td>17</td><td>1.000</td><td>0.941</td><td>0.882</td><td>0.824</td><td>0.765</td><td>0.706</td><td>0.647</td><td>0.588</td></tr>
<tr><td>16</td><td>1.000</td><td>0.938</td><td>0.875</td><td>0.813</td><td>0.750</td><td>0.688</td><td>0.625</td><td>0.563</td></tr>
<tr><td>15</td><td>1.000</td><td>0.933</td><td>0.867</td><td>0.800</td><td>0.733</td><td>0.667</td><td>0.600</td><td>0.533</td></tr>
<tr><td>14</td><td>1.000</td><td>0.929</td><td>0.857</td><td>0.786</td><td>0.714</td><td>0.643</td><td>0.571</td><td>0.500</td></tr>
<tr><td>13</td><td>1.000</td><td>0.923</td><td>0.846</td><td>0.769</td><td>0.692</td><td>0.615</td><td>0.538</td><td>0.462</td></tr>
<tr><td>12</td><td>1.000</td><td>0.917</td><td>0.833</td><td>0.750</td><td>0.667</td><td>0.583</td><td>0.500</td><td>0.417</td></tr>
<tr><td>11</td><td>1.000</td><td>0.909</td><td>0.818</td><td>0.727</td><td>0.636</td><td>0.545</td><td>0.455</td><td>0.364</td></tr>
<tr><td>10</td><td>1.000</td><td>0.900</td><td>0.800</td><td>0.700</td><td>0.600</td><td>0.500</td><td>0.400</td><td>0.300</td></tr>
</table>

Number of shots against

Save Percentage

* A save percentage greater than 0.900 is a sign of a good game.

Overall assessment of the game**

Goals against	Period Played		
	1	2	3
0	6	9	12
1	4	6	8
2	0	2	4
3	-2	-1	0
4	-4	-3	-2
5	-7	-5	-4
6	-10	-7	-6
7	-14	-10	-8
8	-18	-13	-10
9	-20	-16	-12
10	-22	-18	-14
Total 1			

Saves	Points
-41	6
36–40	5
31–35	4
26–30	3
21–25	2
16–20	1
−15	0
Total 2	

Overall assessment of the game
Total 1 + Total 2 =

** A total greater than 4 is a sign of a good game.

Game Observation Sheet

Teams: _____ against _____

Date: _____ Goalie: _____

Shots*:

Direct shot: DS

Rebound shot: R

Deflected shot: D

Deke shot: Dk

* Indicate where the goal was scored using the corresponding letter

* Indicate the origin of the goal using the corresponding letter

Observation about each goal scored:

Calculation of the Save Percentage *

Number of shots against	Number of goals against							
	0	1	2	3	4	5	6	7
50	1.000	0.980	0.960	0.940	0.920	0.900	0.880	0.860
49	1.000	0.980	0.959	0.939	0.918	0.898	0.878	0.857
48	1.000	0.979	0.958	0.938	0.917	0.896	0.875	0.854
47	1.000	0.979	0.957	0.936	0.915	0.894	0.872	0.851
46	1.000	0.978	0.957	0.935	0.913	0.891	0.870	0.848
45	1.000	0.978	0.956	0.933	0.911	0.889	0.867	0.844
44	1.000	0.977	0.955	0.932	0.909	0.886	0.864	0.841
43	1.000	0.977	0.953	0.930	0.907	0.884	0.860	0.837
42	1.000	0.976	0.952	0.929	0.905	0.881	0.857	0.833
41	1.000	0.976	0.951	0.927	0.902	0.878	0.854	0.829
40	1.000	0.975	0.950	0.925	0.900	0.875	0.850	0.825
39	1.000	0.974	0.949	0.923	0.897	0.872	0.846	0.821
38	1.000	0.974	0.947	0.921	0.895	0.868	0.842	0.816
37	1.000	0.973	0.946	0.919	0.892	0.865	0.838	0.811
36	1.000	0.972	0.944	0.917	0.889	0.861	0.833	0.806
35	1.000	0.971	0.943	0.914	0.886	0.857	0.829	0.800
34	1.000	0.971	0.941	0.912	0.882	0.853	0.824	0.794
33	1.000	0.970	0.939	0.909	0.879	0.848	0.818	0.788
32	1.000	0.969	0.938	0.906	0.875	0.844	0.813	0.781
31	1.000	0.968	0.935	0.903	0.871	0.839	0.806	0.774
30	1.000	0.967	0.933	0.900	0.867	0.833	0.800	0.767
29	1.000	0.966	0.931	0.897	0.862	0.828	0.793	0.759
28	1.000	0.964	0.929	0.893	0.857	0.821	0.786	0.750
27	1.000	0.963	0.926	0.889	0.852	0.815	0.778	0.741
26	1.000	0.962	0.923	0.885	0.846	0.808	0.769	0.731
25	1.000	0.960	0.920	0.880	0.840	0.800	0.760	0.720
24	1.000	0.958	0.917	0.875	0.833	0.792	0.750	0.708
23	1.000	0.957	0.913	0.870	0.826	0.783	0.739	0.696
22	1.000	0.955	0.909	0.864	0.818	0.773	0.727	0.682
21	1.000	0.952	0.905	0.857	0.810	0.762	0.714	0.667
20	1.000	0.950	0.900	0.850	0.800	0.750	0.700	0.650
19	1.000	0.947	0.895	0.842	0.789	0.737	0.684	0.632
18	1.000	0.944	0.889	0.833	0.778	0.722	0.667	0.611
17	1.000	0.941	0.882	0.824	0.765	0.706	0.647	0.588
16	1.000	0.938	0.875	0.813	0.750	0.688	0.625	0.563
15	1.000	0.933	0.867	0.800	0.733	0.667	0.600	0.533
14	1.000	0.929	0.857	0.786	0.714	0.643	0.571	0.500
13	1.000	0.923	0.846	0.769	0.692	0.615	0.538	0.462
12	1.000	0.917	0.833	0.750	0.667	0.583	0.500	0.417
11	1.000	0.909	0.818	0.727	0.636	0.545	0.455	0.364
10	1.000	0.900	0.800	0.700	0.600	0.500	0.400	0.300
	Save Percentage							

* A save percentage greater than 0.900 is a sign of a good game.

Overall assessment of the game**

Goals against	Period Played		
	1	2	3
0	6	9	12
1	4	6	8
2	0	2	4
3	-2	-1	0
4	-4	-3	-2
5	-7	-5	-4
6	-10	-7	-6
7	-14	-10	-8
8	-18	-13	-10
9	-20	-16	-12
10	-22	-18	-14
Total 1			

Saves	Points
-41	6
36–40	5
31–35	4
26–30	3
21–25	2
16–20	1
−15	0
Total 2	

Overall assessment of the game
Total 1 + Total 2 =

** A total greater than 4 is a sign of a good game.

Game Observation Sheet

Teams: _____ against _____

Date: _____ Goalie: _____

Shots*:

Direct shot: DS

Rebound shot: R

Deflected shot: D

Deke shot: Dk

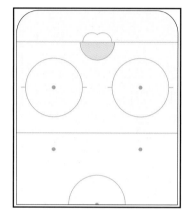

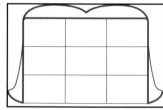

* Indicate the origin of the goal using the corresponding letter

* Indicate where the goal was scored using the corresponding letter

Observation about each goal scored:

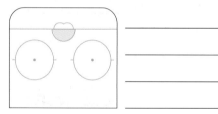 _____
_____
_____

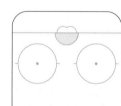 _____
_____
_____

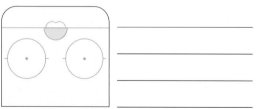 _____
_____
_____

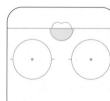 _____
_____
_____

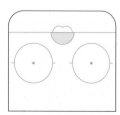 _____
_____
_____

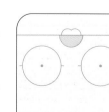 _____
_____
_____

Calculation of the Save Percentage *

	Number of goals against							
	0	1	2	3	4	5	6	7
50	1.000	0.980	0.960	0.940	0.920	0.900	0.880	0.860
49	1.000	0.980	0.959	0.939	0.918	0.898	0.878	0.857
48	1.000	0.979	0.958	0.938	0.917	0.896	0.875	0.854
47	1.000	0.979	0.957	0.936	0.915	0.894	0.872	0.851
46	1.000	0.978	0.957	0.935	0.913	0.891	0.870	0.848
45	1.000	0.978	0.956	0.933	0.911	0.889	0.867	0.844
44	1.000	0.977	0.955	0.932	0.909	0.886	0.864	0.841
43	1.000	0.977	0.953	0.930	0.907	0.884	0.860	0.837
42	1.000	0.976	0.952	0.929	0.905	0.881	0.857	0.833
41	1.000	0.976	0.951	0.927	0.902	0.878	0.854	0.829
40	1.000	0.975	0.950	0.925	0.900	0.875	0.850	0.825
39	1.000	0.974	0.949	0.923	0.897	0.872	0.846	0.821
38	1.000	0.974	0.947	0.921	0.895	0.868	0.842	0.816
37	1.000	0.973	0.946	0.919	0.892	0.865	0.838	0.811
36	1.000	0.972	0.944	0.917	0.889	0.861	0.833	0.806
35	1.000	0.971	0.943	0.914	0.886	0.857	0.829	0.800
34	1.000	0.971	0.941	0.912	0.882	0.853	0.824	0.794
33	1.000	0.970	0.939	0.909	0.879	0.848	0.818	0.788
32	1.000	0.969	0.938	0.906	0.875	0.844	0.813	0.781
31	1.000	0.968	0.935	0.903	0.871	0.839	0.806	0.774
30	1.000	0.967	0.933	0.900	0.867	0.833	0.800	0.767
29	1.000	0.966	0.931	0.897	0.862	0.828	0.793	0.759
28	1.000	0.964	0.929	0.893	0.857	0.821	0.786	0.750
27	1.000	0.963	0.926	0.889	0.852	0.815	0.778	0.741
26	1.000	0.962	0.923	0.885	0.846	0.808	0.769	0.731
25	1.000	0.960	0.920	0.880	0.840	0.800	0.760	0.720
24	1.000	0.958	0.917	0.875	0.833	0.792	0.750	0.708
23	1.000	0.957	0.913	0.870	0.826	0.783	0.739	0.696
22	1.000	0.955	0.909	0.864	0.818	0.773	0.727	0.682
21	1.000	0.952	0.905	0.857	0.810	0.762	0.714	0.667
20	1.000	0.950	0.900	0.850	0.800	0.750	0.700	0.650
19	1.000	0.947	0.895	0.842	0.789	0.737	0.684	0.632
18	1.000	0.944	0.889	0.833	0.778	0.722	0.667	0.611
17	1.000	0.941	0.882	0.824	0.765	0.706	0.647	0.588
16	1.000	0.938	0.875	0.813	0.750	0.688	0.625	0.563
15	1.000	0.933	0.867	0.800	0.733	0.667	0.600	0.533
14	1.000	0.929	0.857	0.786	0.714	0.643	0.571	0.500
13	1.000	0.923	0.846	0.769	0.692	0.615	0.538	0.462
12	1.000	0.917	0.833	0.750	0.667	0.583	0.500	0.417
11	1.000	0.909	0.818	0.727	0.636	0.545	0.455	0.364
10	1.000	0.900	0.800	0.700	0.600	0.500	0.400	0.300

Number of shots against

Save Percentage

* A save percentage greater than 0.900 is a sign of a good game.

Overall assessment of the game**

Goals against	Period Played		
	1	2	3
0	6	9	12
1	4	6	8
2	0	2	4
3	-2	-1	0
4	-4	-3	-2
5	-7	-5	-4
6	-10	-7	-6
7	-14	-10	-8
8	-18	-13	-10
9	-20	-16	-12
10	-22	-18	-14
Total 1			

Saves	Points
-41	6
36–40	5
31–35	4
26–30	3
21–25	2
16–20	1
–15	0
Total 2	

Overall assessment of the game
Total 1 + Total 2 =

** A total greater than 4 is a sign of a good game.

Game Observation Sheet

Teams: _____ against _____

Date: _____ Goalie: _____

Shots*:

Direct shot: DS

Rebound shot: R

Deflected shot: D

Deke shot: Dk

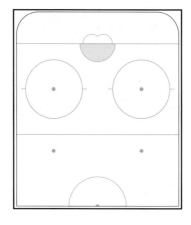

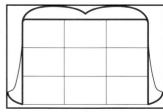

* Indicate the origin of the goal using the corresponding letter

* Indicate where the goal was scored using the corresponding letter

Observation about each goal scored:

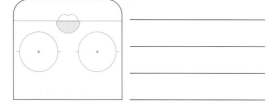 _____
_____
_____
_____

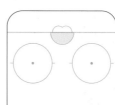 _____
_____
_____
_____

 _____
_____
_____
_____

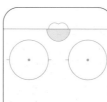 _____
_____
_____
_____

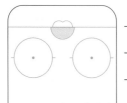 _____
_____
_____

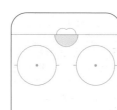 _____
_____
_____

Calculation of the Save Percentage *

Number of shots against	Number of goals against: 0	1	2	3	4	5	6	7
50	1.000	0.980	0.960	0.940	0.920	0.900	0.880	0.860
49	1.000	0.980	0.959	0.939	0.918	0.898	0.878	0.857
48	1.000	0.979	0.958	0.938	0.917	0.896	0.875	0.854
47	1.000	0.979	0.957	0.936	0.915	0.894	0.872	0.851
46	1.000	0.978	0.957	0.935	0.913	0.891	0.870	0.848
45	1.000	0.978	0.956	0.933	0.911	0.889	0.867	0.844
44	1.000	0.977	0.955	0.932	0.909	0.886	0.864	0.841
43	1.000	0.977	0.953	0.930	0.907	0.884	0.860	0.837
42	1.000	0.976	0.952	0.929	0.905	0.881	0.857	0.833
41	1.000	0.976	0.951	0.927	0.902	0.878	0.854	0.829
40	1.000	0.975	0.950	0.925	0.900	0.875	0.850	0.825
39	1.000	0.974	0.949	0.923	0.897	0.872	0.846	0.821
38	1.000	0.974	0.947	0.921	0.895	0.868	0.842	0.816
37	1.000	0.973	0.946	0.919	0.892	0.865	0.838	0.811
36	1.000	0.972	0.944	0.917	0.889	0.861	0.833	0.806
35	1.000	0.971	0.943	0.914	0.886	0.857	0.829	0.800
34	1.000	0.971	0.941	0.912	0.882	0.853	0.824	0.794
33	1.000	0.970	0.939	0.909	0.879	0.848	0.818	0.788
32	1.000	0.969	0.938	0.906	0.875	0.844	0.813	0.781
31	1.000	0.968	0.935	0.903	0.871	0.839	0.806	0.774
30	1.000	0.967	0.933	0.900	0.867	0.833	0.800	0.767
29	1.000	0.966	0.931	0.897	0.862	0.828	0.793	0.759
28	1.000	0.964	0.929	0.893	0.857	0.821	0.786	0.750
27	1.000	0.963	0.926	0.889	0.852	0.815	0.778	0.741
26	1.000	0.962	0.923	0.885	0.846	0.808	0.769	0.731
25	1.000	0.960	0.920	0.880	0.840	0.800	0.760	0.720
24	1.000	0.958	0.917	0.875	0.833	0.792	0.750	0.708
23	1.000	0.957	0.913	0.870	0.826	0.783	0.739	0.696
22	1.000	0.955	0.909	0.864	0.818	0.773	0.727	0.682
21	1.000	0.952	0.905	0.857	0.810	0.762	0.714	0.667
20	1.000	0.950	0.900	0.850	0.800	0.750	0.700	0.650
19	1.000	0.947	0.895	0.842	0.789	0.737	0.684	0.632
18	1.000	0.944	0.889	0.833	0.778	0.722	0.667	0.611
17	1.000	0.941	0.882	0.824	0.765	0.706	0.647	0.588
16	1.000	0.938	0.875	0.813	0.750	0.688	0.625	0.563
15	1.000	0.933	0.867	0.800	0.733	0.667	0.600	0.533
14	1.000	0.929	0.857	0.786	0.714	0.643	0.571	0.500
13	1.000	0.923	0.846	0.769	0.692	0.615	0.538	0.462
12	1.000	0.917	0.833	0.750	0.667	0.583	0.500	0.417
11	1.000	0.909	0.818	0.727	0.636	0.545	0.455	0.364
10	1.000	0.900	0.800	0.700	0.600	0.500	0.400	0.300
Save Percentage								

* A save percentage greater than 0.900 is a sign of a good game.

Overall assessment of the game**

Goals against	Period Played: 1	2	3
0	6	9	12
1	4	6	8
2	0	2	4
3	-2	-1	0
4	-4	-3	-2
5	-7	-5	-4
6	-10	-7	-6
7	-14	-10	-8
8	-18	-13	-10
9	-20	-16	-12
10	-22	-18	-14
Total 1			

Saves	Points
-41	6
36–40	5
31–35	4
26–30	3
21–25	2
16–20	1
–15	0
Total 2	

Overall assessment of the game	
Total 1 + Total 2 =	

** A total greater than 4 is a sign of a good game.